It's Bad News When the Bartender Cries

Dennis Rogers

The News and Observer

Raleigh, N.C.

Also by Dennis Rogers:
Home Grown
Second Harvest
Crossroads

Cover photograph by John Rottet

Artwork by Keith Simmons
Cover design by Dot Stell

For my mother and father, Daisy and Earl Rogers. You lived and loved and laughed and died, all before I knew you. But your dreams and mine came true. I think you would have liked that.

Dennis Rogers on the trail of a story

Contents

About the Book's Author   ix

About the Book's Title   xi

To Live and Die in Dixie   1

The Lawn Warriors   15

Suicide of a Mule   26

Johnny Comes Marching Home   43

The Biscuit War   55

It's Bad News When . . .   80

Time for Nostalgia   104

Once Upon a Two-Stick Popsicle   134

Smuggler's Blues   154

Time to Save the Nauga   174

About the Book's Author

How many columnists does it take to change a light bulb?

Two. One to change the bulb, one to start an argument about how much brighter his bulb is.

If columnists' egos were barbells, not even those East German guys that are about half-German, half-steroid could lift them. The fact is that writing a newspaper column — while it is a back breaker of a job equivalent in wordage to about two novels a year — is as close to being a rock star as an average 45-year-old, underweight boy from Wilson, North Carolina, can get.

This brings me — and a nice segue it was, too — to Dennis Rogers. Dennis has been described before as looking like a fellow who was carved out of a gnarled tree, and that's not bad. I would add that the carver was probably hung over from cheap booze during the Rogers creation, as things are a little, well, uneven all the way around. What there is of it. As country singer Del Reeves once said, "If it weren't for his wallet, he wouldn't have no figure a-tall."

Dennis has been columnist for The News and Observer for 11 years. Column years are to newspapering like dog years are to humans. In 11 years, Dennis has had about 50 years worth of Kiwanis Club speeches, 75 years of barbecue judging, 85 years of beauty pageants and being a "local celebrity" and 125 years worth of words.

I must say he is none the worse for wear. I attribute this to his lovely wife Gail, a good woman of obvious patience. When I first met the boy, I was a columnist for the Greensboro News & Record, and every time I saw Dennis he was wearing jeans and talking about motorcycles while hanging his south end on a northbound bar stool. Now I write editorials for The News and Observer and Dennis lives in a clean house, owns a Yuppie car and wears a tie to work quite often.

This has caused great sadness on the part of his fellow columnists, who regard themselves as a breed apart and, while they may indeed own homes and have children and even play tennis, like to fancy themselves as non-conformists. Most of them, friends, are average guys — and after a few beers, somewhat below average.

Dennis — and I, old buddy, do not consider this a compliment— is as civilized as they come, which is a lot like saying that a $500 used car is "transportation." Nonetheless, he is funny and can hold his liquor, which may be the two most important qualities in getting a man through this life.

This book collects some columns chosen by Dennis and our colleague Guy Munger as the finest of Rogers' recent efforts. I know that some of you are thinking, "Why should I buy a book of stuff that I already read in the paper for a quarter?"

Well ... uh ... the paper is good stock. ... Medium-sized books are hard to find and fill in nicely between Shakespeare and Steinbeck on the bookshelf. ... It will hold down the paper napkins if the fan hits 'em. ... You'd probably have spent the money on something even more foolish. ...

And there's not a word in here about Elvis.

— JIM JENKINS

About the Book's Title

There was deep gloom at the dying 42nd Street Tavern that day and I had been summoned for the wake.

I walked into the oldest continuously operating beer joint in North Carolina expecting to hear the worst. There was a rumor going around that a rich guy had bought the joint. The barflies were saying he was going to tear it down and build a ritzy restaurant where the prices would be high and the patrons well behaved. It was a dismal prospect.

B-Square was behind the bar that day, drunk as a coot. And he was crying.

I did not have to ask. It's bad news when the bartender cries.

I left the 42nd Street Tavern with a column and the title of this book that day in the summer of 1985. The column was one of the more than 2,500 that have occupied the space at the bottom of the third section of The News and Observer since that cold January morning in 1977 when I woke up and found myself with a new job. It was not a job I'd sought, and I was not sure I wanted it, but when I rolled out of Raleigh that day in search of something to write about, I knew things would never be the same. And I was right.

The book you are holding is the fourth collection of columns that have been rescued from the bottom of the bird cage and preserved between hard covers. This collection covers the years from 1984 to 1988 and we've tried to save the best 100 or so columns from the 1,000 that ran during that time. Having one out of 10 that are worth saving is not too bad, I suppose.

I do not use the pronoun "we" out of some inflated sense of my own importance. The only people entitled to call themselves "we" are kings, editors and pregnant women and I am none of the above. But "we" did this one.

Guy Munger edited the book. That means I handed him a stack of columns I liked and told him to make me a book. Then I stayed out of the way and let him worry about the aggravating nit-picking details. He is a fine, dear friend and I value and trust his judgment.

Jack Andrews is a serious Carolina fan and is vice president in charge of a lot of things around here, including books. He wanted the cover to be Carolina Blue but gave in graciously, even

xi

though State Red makes him cringe. He knows when to say yes.

Liz Kelly and Cindy Hinkle have been in charge of getting the book printed, distributed and sold. Their enthusiasm is contagious and welcome. They seem to know just when to smile.

Photographer John Rottet took an off the cuff — and last minute — idea of what I thought I wanted and the result is the photograph on the cover, shot one Sunday morning at dawn. Artist Dot Stell brought the cover to life with her graphics. Dwane Powell, my talented buddy for a lot of years, did the cartoon. I still may sue him.

But while a book springs from the minds and hearts of those who produce it, it ultimately belongs to the readers who spend their hard-earned money to buy it. Once these words were mine, but now they are yours and I hope you got your money's worth.

— DENNIS ROGERS

To Live and Die in Dixie

It is a place of exquisite beauty and diversity. It is a place with native foods so unusual that experts come from afar to savor and explain them. It is a place where accolades are so common as to be greeted with indifference. It is a place where seekers come and want to stay.

Believers will call this a love song and sing along; cynics will sneer and call it myopic boosterism; the defeated will wonder how they missed out. But me, I like Eastern North Carolina.

Long said to be "a valley of humility between two mountains of conceit," North Carolina is romping and stomping toward the 21st century at the top of the heap. We have let others do our bragging for us in recent years, which surely is the seemly way to do it, and we no longer take much notice when yet another group somewhere else picks our place as the best or the fastest-growing or the most fertile to the soul.

But let us now toot our own horn.

What does it take to make a good place? It should look good, shouldn't it? It should have places that cause even the most jaded to take a deep look from time to time.

Some morning when you feel good, get up early and make the dawn run from Morehead City to Cedar Island to catch the 7 a.m. ferry to Ocracoke. The best way to do it is on a motorcycle, but do it any way you can. Roll down the windows and savor the sea breeze and the aroma of new life from the great salt marshes that stretch to the horizon. Give yourself plenty of time. The map says it's 41 miles and you don't want to rush.

There is something good and honest about a place where the mayor of the capital city, a boom town picked as the fastest growing in America, is an ordinary service station owner, and where the governor of the state races his own sailboat and usually loses.

Enough of federally funded $800 hammers and $4,000 ashtrays on warplanes. Walk along the Fayetteville Street Mall in Raleigh at noon on a spring day during ArtsPlosure and watch junior high school students dance gracefully on tax-paid stones. Sit by the tax-paid Beaufort docks at sunset, or walk the tax-paid Wilmington waterfront on a moonlit night, and you know that not all government is shabby and a rip-off.

Grab "two all the way" with the working men one day at Thornton's Lunch in Four Oaks, the place with the neon "Good Eats" sign out front that tells the gospel truth. Have a slow breakfast with Joe Curry at the Murchison House bed-and-breakfast inn in Wilmington, and you've tasted the good life.

We make things, and we make them well. The men and women at the Firestone tire plant in Wilson leave work with almost a cocky swagger at the end of their shift. Is there a better boat than a Hatteras yacht? The peanuts of the fertile northeast, the fat yams and tobacco from all over and the turkeys of the southeast are world-famous.

We make major films in Wilmington. The N.C. Symphony is not too uppity to play honky-tonk music on a Saturday night with a home-grown country band, and almost every town, even little Oriental, has a community theater. Weekend festivals celebrate oysters, crabs, mullet, shrimp and spots.

It is a free and lively place where the people are heard when they argue about schools in Rocky Mount or nuclear power plants in Wake County. But it is a democratic and gentle place where people get mad when politics turn too ugly. The great sweeps of farmland where distant tractors raise rooster tails of dust; the dark, forbidding swamps; the small towns dozing in the afternoon sun; the rolling surf and the windswept beaches where you can walk on sand with almost no footprints — all of these are North Carolina.

It is no wonder we finally have been discovered by the rest of the world. The only mystery is why it took so long. The only question is: How do we keep it?

Y'all be proud of your accents, y'hear?

I am not here to defend the Southern accent against those who would have us sound like we all came from Indiana.

I am not here to self-righteously claim that the slow Suthun drawl is preferable to the nasal twang of Joisey, to da dems, dese and dose of da Bronx, to the flattened vowels of Bahston.

I am not here to act as an interpreter for those natives of other regions who migrate to our fair clime only to discover that they cannot understand a word they hear. For that is their responsibility, not mine. The Frenchman in Paris has no responsibility to speak English when confronted by a gaggle of tourists from Grand Rapids, Mich.

Nor do I wish that our welcomed friends from other places would turn in their accents along with their baggage claim checks when they get off the bus.

I come before you to plead for understanding, for differences, for uniqueness.

In other words, sound like you dang well want to and be proud of it and don't let some smart-mouth tell you otherwise. So there.

What started all this was an article about a speech pathologist in Chattanooga, Tenn., named Beverly Inman-Ebel. Ms. Inman-Ebel is teaching a class called "Success Without the Southern Accent."

Need I say more? Get the grits out of your mouth by signing up for her $65 course at Chattanooga State Technical College and sound like you came from nowhere.

Many of my fellow columnists of the Southern persuasion have taken Ms. Inman-Ebel to task for daring to tinker with the speech of their beloved South, but I do not join them in their pillory. A Southern accent is no better or worse than a clipped English accent, but it is better than no accent at all.

We lose more than a diphthong or two when we cast off the language of our homeland in favor of some prepackaged, freeze-dried, tasteless tongue.

We become like franchised food.

A Big Mac from the McDonald's in Atlantic Beach tastes just like a Big Mac in Seattle; a bowl of Wendy's chili is the same from sea to shining sea; the purple mountain's majesty affects a Burger King Whopper not at all.

We are losing our priceless identity in the relentless cross-country migration that sends us dashing hither and yon in search of the rainbow's end.

Am I wrong in feeling that when you wake up in the morning in Topeka, Kan., you ought to know it? Should the Holiday Inn in Bangor, Maine, feel like the Holiday Inn in St. Louis?

There was a time when you knew where you were in America. You could tell by the food, by the stores, by the hotels, by the way the guy on the radio sounded, by the shape of the highway signs, by the way people dressed and talked and cut their hair.

You might not like what you saw, heard and tasted, but you sure knew you weren't at home, and that was part of the charm.

The franchising of America has not taken over everything yet. Barbecue, thank the Lord, is different all over the country. I brag on ours because it is the best. But I wouldn't want to change the way they do it in Texas; I wouldn't want the legendary ribs of Kansas City to be doused in vinegar and pepper; and even South Carolina, with that mustard sauce stuff, has the duty to keep the regional faith.

To change your accent on purpose is to deny your land and your people. To decry another man's accent is to denigrate his heritage.

People from New York City darn well ought not to sound like people from West Jefferson. And people from Stumpy Point ought not to sound like they came from Des Moines, Iowa.

We came from all over the world to populate this nice chunk of real estate. We brought our distinctive patterns of speech, our customs, our food and our music.

We proudly call America a melting pot, but that is the wrong image. We became vegetable soup. We each added our own bit of flavor to the meal but we each remained distinctive.

I've got a Southern accent. I have friends with a Tex-Mex flavor to their voices, friends who come from Manhattan, N.Y., friends from the Midwest, friends from the Orient. All of us sound like who we are and where we come from when we speak alone. But when our voices ring out and blend in friendly conversation, it sounds like America to me.

Something in the Southern Soul

Franklinton

There is something different about Southerners, a difference that is often inexplicable and can be frustrating and infuriating to Northerners who have moved South.

Part of it — the part they find hardest to understand — is our unending passion for our history, especially the history of The War.

The War Between the States ended more than a century ago, but the memories of it live as strongly among some Southerners as if they had been there and had fought it. We still honor the memory of the men who fought for that lost and noble cause and we still honor the flag under which they fought.

In recent years, however, that battle flag has been besmirched by those who would make it a symbol of racial hatred. It is a link to a past that many Northerners don't understand or like. It is ancient history, they say. It is over, they say. You can't keep fighting the war, they say.

And they are wrong. Even we who do it often don't understand why we do it. But something binds us to that past. There is something in the Southern soul that will not let it go.

Thilbert Pearce was just a child when his father would take him down to the old Franklinton Hotel to see the old men as they gathered each year.

"I thought they were an extremely dignified group of elderly gentlemen in their old uniforms," he remembers. "It made a tremendous impression on me."

The old men who gathered each year were veterans of the War for Southern Independence, or if you prefer, the War of the Rebellion. But never call it the "Civil War" when Thilbert Pearce is around.

"It was not a civil war," says Pearce, who has made a lifelong study of the war years. "There was nothing civil about it. No one was trying to overthrow the government, which is what a civil war is.

"The North called it the 'War of the Rebellion' and the Southern veterans called it the 'War for Southern Independence.' It wasn't until this century that people started calling it the Civil War. It was no more a civil war than the American Revolution had been less than 100 years earlier. It was the same thing: a group of people trying to break away and start a new country. It was a revolution, but it was not a civil war."

Pearce, 66 and a lifelong resident of Franklin County, is serious about his Southern roots and his war research. He has written numerous books and articles on the period and has a private library that would rival that of any public or school library. His speciality is Franklin County's role in the war.

"This county had a population of about 6,000 people," he said. "And more than 1,400 men and boys from here served in the war and more than 400 were lost. You take 400 men, the cream of the crop, out of a county this size and the impact is tremendous. There were a lot of widows left after that war. My great-great-grandfather was killed at Sharpesburg and my great-great-grandmother was killed in an accident right after the war. They left six orphans to be taken care of at the worst possible time in history. They lost everything."

Pearce is not a saber-rattling, never-give-up-the-fight, die-hard Rebel. Yet, when he talks about the war, it is obvious that what happened to his ancestors and his homeland still has an emotional impact. His eyes seem to look off to a distant battlefield and his voice grows soft and serious. He is a Southern man and he still carries the collective memories of his people in his heart.

"The war is still important to Southerners," he said. "There is no way to explain that to Northerners. They would never understand. You can't explain it to them and you don't have to explain it to Southerners. So I don't even try anymore.

"But Southerners are different. Although other people are resentful of the fact that we're proud to be Southerners, look at who is first to volunteer when there is a war. We are loyal Americans. But we are Southern-Americans first in a way that Midwesterners would never be."

Perhaps, Thilbert agrees, part of the difference is that our land is the only American land ever to be invaded successfully by an enemy army. And we are descendants of the only army of Americans ever defeated in war on our own soil.

Our heritage, as difficult as it might be for others to understand, is important to Southerners and, as long as historians like Thilbert Pearce are around to remind us of it, it will never be forgotten. We are what we are today because of that heritage, not in spite of it, and I think that's a pretty good thing to be.

For the discriminating Dixie diner

Here's how it works.

There are thousands of people in the country whose job it is to get their clients' names or products favorably mentioned in newspapers.

They are public relations people. We in the news media tend to call them flacks. Often we ignore what they send us, but sometimes they do get our attention.

That is why this piece is about Moon Pies. Somebody mailed me a box of Moon Pies in the hope that I would mention a new book called "The Great American Moon Pie Handbook," written by Ron Dickson of Charlotte.

The book is fine but the Moon Pies were wonderful. I grabbed one of those delectables and almost got run over by the horde of reporters and editors who were hot on the scent. Foolishly, I did not even save one for the boss, and he let me know it.

I had planned to enjoy my Moon Pies in secret and never mention a word about them. But, darn it all, they were Double Decker Deluxe Moon Pies, so I felt obliged.

Moon Pies certainly need no help from me. They have been the official snack food of Southerners accustomed to fine dining for 66 years now, and their popularity is undiminished. In fact, Moon Pies are spreading coast to coast.

I know there are, at most, no more than five people in North Carolina who have never tasted a Moon Pie. And they probably would not admit it. But for those few, this is a Moon Pie:

It comes out of Chattanooga, Tenn., by way of every decent country store and vending machine in the South. The basic Moon Pie is made of two soft cookies that are a little like graham crackers. The middle is filled with a soft, snowy marshmallow cream. The cookies are dipped in chocolate. The whole thing is stuck together and wrapped in cellophane. It is four inches in diameter.

Looking back over those meager words, it occurs to me that that description is like saying the Mona Lisa is a picture and Richard Petty is a car driver.

Moon Pies are easy to recognize. They feature a smiling yellow crescent moon on the package and carry the immortal words: "The Original Marshmallow Sandwich." Do not be fooled by imitations.

The Moon Pie's place in the rural South is an honored one. Traditionally, the boss man brings a snack to the field hands about 9:30 or 10 a.m., sort of a redneck tea time. Traditionally, that snack is a big soft drink and a Moon Pie.

(Just recently, for example, the brave men fighting the stubborn fires in the Albemarle-Pamlico peninsula were gobbling scores of Moon Pies every day.)

You will not be looked at with more than passing interest if you go into a country store and buy a couple of boxes of Moon Pies at the time. You will be thought of as a kindly boss man.

The sugar rush from a 16 oz. soft drink (Nehi Orange is so good) and a Moon Pie is awesome. Spirits are lifted, loads get lighter and the rows get shorter when fueled with these taste sensations.

The bean-sprouts-for-lunch bunch probably would not approve of Moon Pies. But listen how smoothly the almost-sensuous ingredients roll off the tongue:

"Corn syrup, flour, sugar, vegetable shortening (contains one or more of the following: partially hydrogenated soybean oil, palm oil, hydrogenated palm oil or hydrogenated cottonseed oil), soy flour, gelatin, leavening (baking soda), cocoa (if appearance indicates), soy lecithin, artificial flavoring, artificial coloring and sodium sulfite."

Yum, yum. And remember, store at room temperature.

Those who have immigrated to our fair Southland may not have had the opportunity or the courage to eat a Moon Pie. If you are one of those and perhaps you are feeling a little homesick or left out when the locals get to talking about barbecue and stock car racing, I have the solution.

Go to your local store and buy a Moon Pie and a big orange drink. In the privacy of your own home, carefully open the Moon Pie by grasping each side of the cellophane package with your thumb and forefinger and gently pulling it apart. Savor the aroma much as you would the bouquet of a fine wine. Gently push the Moon Pie up until it clears the wrapper.

Then gobble it down in large bites alternating with swallows of drink. Ignore the crumbs until you are finished and then — delicately, please — moisten the end of one finger, pick up the crumbs and eat them.

You will feel at home.

No Cure for Tobacco Nostalgia

A new one probably hasn't been built in 25 years, and the old ones are falling in, but tobacco barns still are the most recognizable feature on the landscape of Eastern North Carolina.

A friend from other parts recently asked me what those thousands of mostly vacant tobacco barns were used for, and I explained how you brought the tobacco to the barn, tied it on sticks and hung it on rafters, where it was cured with heat for several days. It emerged dry and golden and was graded and then taken to market to sell.

Later, I realized what an inadequate explanation that was. That's like saying home is a place where you sleep and eat.

Tobacco barns were the center of life on a farm. Replaced now by look-alike metal bulk barns, once they were the places where you spent more time than you did at home. You ate, slept, worked, loved and fought there. And when the season ended, it was the site of the biggest party of the year.

Curing tobacco in those barns was a mystic science. You had to raise and lower the heat several times during the three- or four-day curing cycle. That meant somebody had to stay at the barn around the clock because a lot of the barns used wood heat and it took a master to keep that fire stoked just right.

Now, a man sitting up all night to keep a constant temperature in a barn has to have something to do to while away the long hours. My Daddy and his friends often spent their nights drinking and playing cards.

They were hard-working men, but when night fell, they liked to take a little drink — and what better place than sitting outside on a summer night? Daddy would have a barn curing, and just after dark, his friends would arrive to keep him company.

They ran a drop cord from the house and hung a bare light bulb over the bench where we tied tobacco. Somebody would pull out a half-gallon jar of white liquor, shake it up to test the bead and pass it around. Somebody else would pull out a dog-eared deck of cards, and they'd play, drink and tell lies until the last of them went home or fell asleep.

One night they made a frog disappear.

They were sitting around as usual, passing the jar, when Daddy noticed that there were a lot of frogs around that night.

He took a 12-gauge shotgun shell — shotguns were kept handy to shoot anything that needed shooting — and gently took it apart with his pocket knife. He poured the powder out and put it in a little pile near the edge of the light and went back and sat down.

A few minutes passed and soon a frog hopped up to that pile of gunpowder and started eating it. I watched in amazement, as did Daddy's barn buddies, as the frog ate all of it.

Once the powder was gone, Daddy went over to the fire and scooped up a single hot coal and rolled it toward the frog. Thinking it was some kind of brilliant bug, the frog tried to eat the hot coal.

The frog disappeared in a loud flash.

The end-of-tobacco-season party was held after the last crop of tobacco had been harvested. Everyone was there — from the white man who drove a Buick and owned the farm, to the tenant farmers who lived there, to the black field hands hired by the day.

Some folks cooked a pig, but we had a catfish stew. The party would start at the barn in the late afternoon when the stew was put on to cook. There were drinking and music and eating and young folks sneaking off behind the barn in search of privacy and a harmless fight or two and talk of crops, neighbors and old times.

It was a time of thanksgiving that we'd made it, for better or worse, for another year. The party would go long into the night and when the sun came up the next morning, a few folks would be sleeping in the back of their pickups with hangovers so bad they were sure they'd have to get better to die.

I remember those tobacco barn parties when I see the old barns that are falling in. I remember Daddy and the frog and the first girl I ever had a crush on. Daddy's dead now, I don't know what happened to the Foley girl from up the road (or her brothers named Temple, Doll and Son), and nobody makes frogs disappear anymore.

Growth Has Its Trade-offs

These things start small, just one little gesture, one little word here and there, and the first thing you know, you've got a full-fledged revolution on your hands.

It may have started already.

At first glance it is no big deal, just a fake license plate that you stick on the front of your car. It looks like a North Carolina license plate but instead of numbers, there is the word "NATIVE."

I saw one, then another, and now I'm seeing them all over the place. They're being sold in convenience stores, mostly in the Raleigh area, and showing up on cars and pickups around town.

What does it all mean? Perhaps nothing, but maybe our highly touted Southern hospitality, of which we are justifiably proud, is wearing just a bit ragged around the edges.

No one would deny that the growth in the Triangle has been good for just about all of us, and just about all of us are glad it happened. We've gone from being a nice but sort of slow-moving and boring Southern town to being a lively and prosperous city. There are more theaters, more restaurants, more concerts, more of just about everything good than there was 10 years ago.

But there is a lot more traffic, fewer country music honky tonks, more finely engineered German luxury cars, fewer trees, more ugly shopping centers, fewer Southern accents; driving to the Research Triangle Park is infinitely more difficult, slower and more frustrating than it was a mere five years ago.

Those who stand to make a fistful of dollars from the exploding growth of Raleigh will tell you everything is wonderful. But I ask you, do we need 16 pages of real estate related companies in the phone book and 21 pages of listings for various things having to do with computers?

What we need are more places to buy good cowboy boots and some Saturday night places to wear them. Most "NATIVE" Southerners have a real soft spot in their heart for country music, but you'd never know it by looking in local record stores. There is a lot more Mozart than Merle Haggard on the shelves.

What are these folks with "NATIVE" plates trying to tell the world? Jimmy Cummings of Raleigh has one on his car and he said, "I don't mind the people moving to Raleigh, but it is getting to the place where you don't feel like you're at home any more. I was born and raised in North Carolina, and I've lived in Raleigh for 20 years, but it doesn't seem like a Southern town any more. You can go to the malls and never hear a Southern accent. I wanted to let people know there are a few of us natives left."

Have we gone one Raleigh-bound moving van, one new

high-tech plant opening, one BMW over the line? Have we reached social gridlock? Are we full?

I hope not, because most of those who have moved to Raleigh have made it a better, more interesting place to live, but Raleigh's charm as a warm, Southern city has been diminished. The sweet flavor that drew so many to our town came from our people and our place, not from the vast, look-alike tracts of North Raleigh and Cary, not from the steady march of shopping centers with names that are beginning to sound alike. They could be anywhere. There is nothing Raleigh about them.

I know, it's the old drawbridge mentality. I'm here, so pull up the bridge so no one else can get in. And there may be something to it. I moved to Raleigh 11 years ago and fell in love with it almost immediately. I hope never to leave it. I have friends, and a wife, who came here from out of state to work and they've stayed and I welcome them.

But like those who sport "NATIVE" plates, I worry about our town. If we grow too much too fast, if we mall it to death, if we destroy the Southern soul of the place, we will have created a new town; and although it may be rich, it won't be Raleigh and it won't be as good. We've got a great goose here who has laid a large number of golden eggs. Let's take care of her.

The "NATIVES" have gone out of their way to make newcomers welcome. Newcomers always tell you that the people here were so friendly that they felt at home right away. But that was before the "NATIVE" license plates showed up.

The "NATIVES" listen to the radio and hear of killings on the Los Angeles freeways while they're stopped in traffic on I-40. They read of the homeless of New York and see more and more hungry people lining up for meals at the downtown missions and churches. They hear their co-workers talk of housing development names they couldn't find with a road map.

They're "NATIVES" and proud of it, but sometimes they feel like strangers in their own town.

GQ meets Bubba's overalls

Guys, let's talk hip. Serious male hipness. Hip, like in Gentleman's Quarterly. Of course, if you're really a hip kind of guy, you call it GQ.

This is a magazine that features male models wearing greasy hair combed straight back so the comb marks show, sport coats with the sleeves pushed up and pensive looks. I'd look pensive, too, if I'd just dropped $350 on a shirt that needs ironing.

In its most recent issue, which I swear on the grave of Hank Williams Sr. is the first one I ever bought, there is an article entitled "99 things every 30-year-old must know."

It says, for instance, that by the time you are 30, you guys should: have bailed a buddy out of jail, have been to half a dozen major league ball parks, have had your heart broken, have had a one night stand you're ashamed of, be able to politely say no to a woman, have thrown out your Aqua Velva, have given up air guitar, have said something to a boss and lover that you'll regret for the rest of your life, and have spent one night in either jail, a bordello, a monastery, a youth hostel or a Motel 6.

It is stuff like that that makes you hip, GQ says.

But this is not hip. This is pretending to be hip. Real Hip is Country Hip. Real Hip is knowing that Hank Williams Jr.'s mama's name was Miss Audrey and being able to sink a two-rail pool shot the long way. Real Hip is Bubba Hip.

It takes a different set of skills and experiences to be Bubba Hip. While GQ insists that to be hip you must own a tuxedo, Bubba says you must own at least one pair of bibbed overalls that you wear without a shirt.

GQ says you should own a power drill by age 30. Bubba says make that a chain saw and not one of those dinky suburban ones either, but a full throttle monster than can cut through a Plymouth.

GQ says 30-year-olds should have had six nights that you could not remember the day after. Bubba says you should wake up at least six mornings and not remember where you left your pickup.

GQ says you should have had one ugly experience with at least one lawyer. Bubba says make that one beautiful experience with an ugly woman, preferably an overweight one.

GQ says you should know how to pronounce "Chassagne-Montrachet and when to drink it." Bubba says you should know how to pronounce "chitterlings" and have the guts not to eat them when those around you are making fools of themselves.

GQ says you should know which is worth more, a flush or a straight, and why. Bubba says if you don't know, you are welcome to play poker with him any time.

GQ says you should own a hat that is not a ski, baseball or

cowboy hat. Bubba says why?

GQ says you should be able to carve a turkey by the time you are 30. Bubba says you should never carve a turkey that you didn't shoot, either in the woods or at the rescue squad's annual fund-raising turkey shoot.

GQ says you should "have used a good one-liner if perchance, God forbid, by some quirk of fate, occasionally you were unable to perform sexually." Bubba has no idea what they're talking about.

GQ says you should have had "an adult sports experience that equals in glory a childhood sports experience." Bubba adds that it should involve shotguns, pool cues or a bored and stroked '66 GTO.

GQ says you must have one restaurant where you are known and still welcome. Bubba says you must have one tavern where you are known — and not welcome.

GQ says you should be able to pick a ripe cantaloupe. Bubba says you should be able to grow a ripe cantaloupe.

GQ says you should, by the time you are 30, have skinny dipped with someone worth bragging about. Bubba says you never swim nekkid with a lady then brag about it.

GQ says you should be able to speak a foreign language by the time you are 30. Bubba says that speaking English is tough enough for him by 11:30 on Saturday night.

GQ says you should be able to hum the entire score of "Guys and Dolls." Bubba says you should be able to complete the following country music lyric: "I was drunk the day my mama got out of prison . . . "

GQ says you should have worn an earring by the time you're 30. Bubba says he thinks he understands the problem with GQ Hip.

The Lawn Warriors

I used to worry about interesting things.

I worried about national defense, the decline of moral values in America and the mechanical threat posed to my motorcycle by unleaded gas. I was concerned about the quality of life in the inner city, acid rain and which singles bar had the best happy hour buffet.

All that has changed. Life in the suburbs has claimed another victim. Now I worry about Japanese beetles.

Let me assure you how little the annual invasion of Japanese beetles has meant to me in past years. As a single man in my inner-city house, I had no bushes of interest to beetles. I would have been more than pleased if a horde of them had descended on the ugly and rapidly growing bushes that hovered menacingly near my old house. It would have been sheer delight to walk out one morning to find that the beetles had reduced the bushes to nude kindling.

But no, Japanese beetles do not care for useless bushes. Japanese beetles are fond of crepe myrtles, an attractive, flowering shrub native to yards that cost a lot of money.

We made it through the spring in fine horticultural fashion in our North Raleigh suburban home. The dogwoods in our yard were spectacular. The azaleas bloomed their hearts out so magnificently that I, an anti-yard work person if there ever was one, went out and bought six more azaleas and planted them with my own non-calloused hands (hooray, only one had gone to azalea heaven). We had some things that looked like tulips and radiated in pure colors. The crab apple turned out to be the prettiest bush I ever saw.

But there were two big bushes out by the street that just sat there and did nothing but get in the way of the lawn mower. I hate cutting grass, and anything that makes it harder is just another reason to postpone the odious job. I considered removing the offending shrubs to make the job easier.

But my wife, who has spent most of her adult years in an apartment reading and dreaming of the day she'd have her own yard to worry about, nay-sayed my idea. Those are crepe myrtles, she said, and they will be beautiful in the summer when they bloom.

My wife — for the first and last time, I trust — lied to me. Those bushes have sat there doing what most bushes do: being fairly ugly and taking up space.

When crepe myrtles are in full bloom — shining pink, purple and white — they are a midsummer delight. But not at our house. The crepe myrtles at our house have become Japanese beetle motels, and there are no vacancies.

Not deterred by this invasion, my wife had declared war on Japanese beetles. With her scientific mind at full throttle, she has installed something called a Bag-a-Bug.

This is an insidious device that, for some reason, makes me philosophically nervous. It does work. She installed it one evening, and by noon the next day, it had rid the world of at least 100 Japanese beetles.

It is very simple. Japanese beetles are romantically inclined to a fault, and this time of the year, the boy beetles are intent on finding a girl beetle to wed and have children.

The Bag-a-Bug works sort of like a singles bar for beetles. It uses something called a sex lure to attract the boy beetles. This is not unlike the perfumes that some ladies splash liberally about their person on date nights, and both of them seem to work.

The boy beetles flock to the lure, and, once they enter to the

Bag-a-Bug to check out the action, they find that it was all a sham, and they die.

Having been in similar situations, I feel a twinge of male guilt about tricking boy beetles like this.

Here they were, their iridescent green and brown shells shining on a summer day and with love on their minds, a few dollars in their beetle pockets and a ready rap to lay on the lady beetles, and what happens? They end up in the bag with hundreds of boy beetles in a similar condition.

At first I thought they were merely stupid. Here was a bag full of hundreds of dead beetles, and these idiots kept coming and joining the crowd. But I have been out there on the hunt myself a time or two, and I have spent many hours and many dollars in similar places full of sweet-smelling ladies and strike-out artists who thought they'd get lucky tonight. The only difference is, we got to try again.

Not so with the beetles of my neighborhood. Many of my neighbors have these Bag-a-Bug things, and together we are all killing thousands of them. And so far this blooming season, exactly one bloom has appeared on the two large crepe myrtles in front of the house. The beetles are the talk of the neighborhoods of North Raleigh, as we compare the size of our beetle kills.

Once I worried about important things. Now I live in the 'burbs and worry about lust-filled beetles.

A mind is a terrible thing to waste.

Three Little Words (Not Those Three)

The news that I was getting married next week drew a lot of comment from my friends.

"Have you lost your mind?" was just one sample comment.

So I feel I should explain why I got married. Shortly before the wedding, my future bride, the lovely and talented Gail Knowlton of the Massachusetts Knowltons, and I were assembling something called a "drop spreader." A drop spreader — for you apartment and condo types — is a little cart with a hole in the bottom that is used to spread fertilizer and grass seed, or so I hope because that's what we are going to do with it. I don't know why they call it a "drop" spreader instead of a "fertilizer" spreader, but that's life in the suburbs.

The drop-spreader thing came in a nice box with three little words on it, three words that have caused me more psychic pain and skinned knuckles than I like to think about. The three little words were "some assembly required."

You would think, wouldn't you, that at the price drop spreaders go for these days, they could at least put them together for you? They don't manufacture drop spreaders anymore; they sell boxes full of drop-spreader parts. You become the manufacturer. Next thing you know they'll be selling shirts with "some assembly required."

We opened the box and looked at the jumble of unrecognizable things in it. I figured out which were the wheels and which were the screws, but the rest of it could just as well have been leftovers from a nuclear plant or a kid's tricycle.

I felt a suburban, macho need to take charge of the drop spreader assembly situation since several of my neighbors-to-be were out in their North Raleigh yards scoping out the new folks down the street. My neighbor across the street was pretending to teach a kid to ride a bicycle — turns out he'd borrowed the kid just to have an excuse to keep an eye on us — and the guy next door was washing a car. But I felt their eyes on me. This was my suburban trial by fire.

"You know, that Rogers can't even build a drop spreader from scratch," I figured they'd be saying as soon as I went in for a bandage. "I don't know if he's going to work out or not. We do have certain standards, you know. A man who can't build a drop spreader is not likely to be much good as a source of borrowed tools." How right they are.

I sat down on the steps to read the eight pages of instructions for building a drop spreader. I once assembled a fully functioning, fully automatic M-16 rifle with instructions printed on a three-by-five card, and that took a long time, so I was sweating a little because we only had three hours of daylight left.

First came tool time. I didn't have mine with me. Darn the luck, I'd left my entire collection of homeowner's tools in my other shirt pocket. However, the lovely and talented Miss Knowlton had her own tools, an entire box of them, a real metal toolbox with a handle and a tray and everything. That is the first reason I'm going to marry her. A woman with her own tools is not a woman to be taken lightly.

She had stunned me already when we installed a new shower head, and the woman had her own tube of the sticky stuff you use to keep the thing from leaking. She didn't have to go buy it; she already had some in her nifty toolbox. I'd never heard of the stuff and she had a tube of it in her toolbox.

I began reading the eight-page instruction sheet while she was humming softly and pawing through the mess of drop-spreader parts in the box with the three little words — "some assembly required" — printed on the side.

Almost as a joke, I read the following words aloud to her, expecting she'd say what I'd say: "Huh?"

"Slide 'T' knob (11) onto stem of tee handle (8); (Fig. 14). Print should face operator as shown in (Fig. 14). Use same procedure for cam knob (12); (Fig. 14). Numbers should face toward 'T' knob. Slide tee handle (8) over control wire (13) until wire exits at slot between cam knob (12) and 'T' knob (11); (Fig. 15). Correct placement requires 'T' knob above and cam knob below exiting control wire."

Do you know what she said when I finished reading that? She said, "What's next? I've already done that."

That is why I married her.

Lawn and Short of Cutting Grass

I've got to hurry up and finish writing this so I can get home.

My grass is growing even as I type. In fact, my grass is growing faster than I can type.

I am just as thrilled as I can be that we're finally getting plenty of rain. Everyone always says the same thing when it rains and spoils their weekends. "Well," they say, "the farmers need the rain. Let us sit here and mildew."

Good for the farmers. I could use a little more sunshine, myself. But have you heard a farmer say, "Well, the people who work in town need some sunshine"? I doubt it.

Goodness knows, the farmers deserve a good year. But come this fall when they're sitting on the porch counting all the money they made, I'm going to be in the hospital from overwork.

I have never seen anything like this summer for grass. We have had ideal growing conditions. Every day has been hot and humid with an inch of rain on my days off each week. My grass is thicker and lusher than ever before. It is growing so well that it is about to strangle the weeds that I normally count on to give my lawn a greenish tint. My lawn, when cut, looks terrific.

I can assure you that was not my idea. I liked the drought. Last year, I cut my grass only about five times. What a great summer.

You may have deduced that I am not a lawn person. I have tried to care, but it is not within me to lie awake at night trying to figure out how to make my lawn one shade greener.

I come by my aversion honestly. Down around Cherry Grove in Columbus County, folks didn't have lawns. We had yards, and we didn't fool with them very much. A yard, generally between the road and the front porch, was a place to park a pickup, not to recreate Eden. Cows ate grass. Man parked on dirt.

I never saw a lawn mower until we moved to town. Yard work consisted of sweeping the yard with a yard broom made out of broom straw. They were homemade affairs in which a handful of broom straw was cut and tied together with twine on the stalk end. About the only reason we ever swept was to get rid of the leaves, which we burned, or to cover oil spills from the Farmall Cub, the leakingest tractor in the world. If a sprig of grass did dare to sprout up, it was immediately eaten by the next horse through the yard.

But city folks didn't have any dirt to play in like we did, so they invented sissy lawns to replace honest yards. Now the influence has spread, and farmers have lawns. As if they didn't already have enough to do.

Mechanization is the villain. Back in the golden days — defined in this case as presubdivision (yes, Virginia, North Raleigh used to be in the country) — folks lived in town with little lots. Drive through Oakwood for an example. The reason was, they had to push their lawn mowers.

It was a pleasant, idyllic time. Birds sang. Children laughed. Folks sat on the porch after supper. Down the block, Mr. Whipple pushed his lawn mower with a steady, even motion. It was a soft, droning sound. Then it all changed.

They moved north to big lots and bought power mowers. Saturday morning in North Raleigh sounds like the starting line at Daytona International Speedway. The screaming engines roar through the Bermuda grass and slash through the centipede. Yards get seeded and fertilized.

Lawn fertilizer is the dumbest idea since lights at a drive-in movie. What idiot puts fertilizer on a lawn to make it grow faster so he has to work even harder? Me, that's who. And now I'm paying the price.

These power mowers changed everything. Now there are no limits. A man's lawn can be as big as his gas tank. Too big to push the power mower? Here's a little number that pushes itself. Tired of just walking behind it? Here, sit down and ride.

Values have become warped. The whole idea of moving to the suburbs was to pretend you were in the country. But the city folks brought their little lawns from the old neighborhoods and spread them all over the place.

Now the people in the country are trying to pretend they're in the city by having manicured lawns around the old place, instead of their old-fashioned country yards.

More of the Perils of Suburbia

We were lolling on the deck late one afternoon, grooving on the spring weather and the dogwoods blooming in the back yard when a startling sight appeared before us.

The cat had turned green.

I was concerned about this. Cats are not supposed to turn green, but French Fry the cat certainly was green. Actually, he was sort of chartreuse, but that is like mauve and puce — color words that should not be used in polite conversation because everyone disagrees about what color they are. So we'll call it green.

Look, my wife said, the cat is green. We had been heatedly discussing international immigration laws (trust me, you don't want to know more about that, and I hate we ever brought it up), and I figured she was just trying to change the subject because she knew I had her on the debating ropes, but sure enough, there it was: a green cat.

I looked around. The cat was not the only thing that had turned green. The top of my rusty grill was green. The rusty folding chairs were green. The rusty tables that used to be white were green. Lord have mercy, my motorcycle was green.

I looked at my wife. She was turning green. She looked at me. I was turning green.

The prehistoric Indians, as usual, had a descriptive phrase for what was happening in my back yard: They called it "molokoca derotic yech," which means: "that nasty chartreuse stuff that comes from the Big Sky and gets all over everything this time of the year."

Scientists have proved that upwards of 17 jillion pounds of yellow-green pine tree pollen will fall in Raleigh this year. Look toward the sun, and you can see it — billowing clouds of nasty powder wafting earthward from the tall pines.

A clerk at a combination gas station, convenience store and automatic car wash in Raleigh mentioned it to me the other day. She said this was her first spring in Raleigh and asked whether I knew what all that yellow stuff (see what I mean, some call chartreuse green, and some call it yellow) was that was all over everything. I told her about the Indians.

"Well, whatever it is," she said. "They're about to wear my automatic car wash out. People are washing their cars every day."

As if that will help.

Yes it is pollen, and yes, newcomers, it will go away in a week or so. But until then, keep the windows closed, don't hang clothes on the line (two mistakes I made in one week) and don't worry about your green cat. They don't have much to do but wash themselves anyway.

No, the big problem is not the pollen. It is the grass.

We had a drought last year, and though it might have been devastating to the farmers, it was pretty good for the lawn owners of North Raleigh, of which I am now one.

I am new to the 'burbs, having spent most of my life in old neighborhoods with old lawns, which means mostly weeds. I figured it didn't matter what the growth was as long as I kept it short. So about every three weeks, I'd shave my lawn down to a pool table finish.

You do that in North Raleigh and the Lawn Vigilantes will get you.

A fellow came to the house one day. He had a big tank truck parked out front, and he had come to give me a deal. He said that four times a year, he'd come and spray my lawn with some stuff that would make the grass grow green and keep the weeds away. I asked him what my choices were, and he said, "You can have a dusty, barren, weed-choked disaster of a yard and all your neighbors will laugh at you, or you can have a lush green lawn that will be the pride of the neighborhood. Sign here."

I did. Now I am cutting my grass every three days. I don't like cutting grass at all, and here I am, paying some man to increase my work load four-fold.

I even bought a grass catcher to fit on the lawn mower I permanently borrowed from a friend last year because every time the spraying man comes, he gives my yard a "thatch test" and I'm afraid I'll flunk if I don't get up all the clippings. I always was an overachiever and hate to flunk tests of any kind.

I've already flunked one North Raleigh Lawn Test. I cut my grass like I always have, real short. No, no, no, my lawn sprayer said. You must cut it no shorter than 3 inches high. He even wrote it on my Lawn Care Report Card. I thought you wanted the grass to look like it has just been cut, but no, like a $20 haircut, you want it to look like it hasn't been cut.

One week, it rained a lot, so I had to wait a whole 10 days between grass cuttings. Big deal. Ten days.

My grass was so high in 10 days that I had to stop to empty the grass catcher every 50 feet, and that meant turning off the lawn mower, taking off the grass catcher, emptying it and then putting it back on and pulling that starter cord three or four times. It was a long day.

Life is sure hard in the 'burbs.

Wanted: Mediator With Swatches

There are a lot of things than can cause trouble in a new marriage, and most people take them into consideration when planning their nuptials.

I like grits and she doesn't. I went to Carolina and she went to State. I'm from the South and she's from the North. I like American cars and she likes imports. I like motorcycles and she'd rather walk. I like big dogs and she quakes at the sight of a Doberman.

But you can work those things out. I've got her to where she likes country music, so all things are possible. But I'm not sure that will be possible with this latest crisis.

It is time to decorate. I don't mean decorate for Christmas. I mean decorate forever, as in sofas and chairs and rugs and stuff.

Truthfully, our house has been looking a bit barren for the past year. It has had all the rustic charm of a fraternity house. You see, I had my stuff when we got married and she had her stuff. I didn't care much for her stuff and she didn't care much for my stuff, but you lie a lot when you are courting so the issue of how to decorate our new house never came up.

We made some compromises when we got married. I gave my daughter most of my living room stuff, and my wife allowed me to keep my sofa, perhaps the most comfortable sofa since they invented sofas, in what we laughingly referred to as the library. I got to put the king-size water bed in our bedroom, and her bed ended up in the guest room. She did try to kill my plastic pink flamingo, but I rescued it in the nick of time.

Her furniture ended up in the living room. It is ugly and it is uncomfortable, but it was expensive and it is pretty much free of food and drink stains, unlike mine. In other words, it is the kind of furniture you'd expect a single, professional woman to have. It is the kind of furniture on which you'd have polite conversations about important topics and behave yourself, unlike mine, which encouraged slouching, eating popcorn, drinking beer from cans and wrestling. You know, guy furniture.

Now it is time, she said, to really fix up the place.

We began with magazines. My wife was nudging 30 when we got married, and for all of her adult life she has been collecting decorating magazines in preparation for the big day when she'd have her own house. They were all in a big box that I thought I had thrown away, but somehow she retrieved it. She opened that big box a couple of weeks ago and proceeded to make me sit down and go through all 3,000 magazines looking at furniture pictures.

It was obvious trouble was coming. I hated everything she liked, and she hated everything I liked. So we brought in a referee.

This referee is an interior decorator, and she charges $45 an hour to keep you from killing each other.

She came to the house last week for a consultation, and I've got to hand it to her. She walked in, took one look around and did not laugh, cry or stalk out. At $45 an hour, I was not interested in making much small talk, and she got right to the point.

I begged for a coffee table on which I could put my feet while watching ACC basketball while wife talked about dining room chairs with curly little feet. I said I liked blue furniture a lot, while my wife waxed on about celery and raspberry, which looked like green and purple to me, but I didn't say anything. I said I wanted to watch TV and the fireplace at the same time, and when the decorator said something about a sectional sofa, I thought my wife would leap up and beat her to death.

The decorator asked me if I liked Queen Anne or Windsor dining room furniture. I felt like I'd just flunked a pop quiz. I said I liked to sit down and eat a long time without my butt getting sore. I don't know if that helped much or not.

I said I wanted some pictures on the wall, and she said she was an art dealer as well. That scared me. I didn't tell her that my goal of pictures on the wall could be met in 20 minutes at the flea market. I decorated my last house with pictures everywhere for under $100 total, and she just smiled the kind of tolerant smile that you save for senile aunts and silly children.

I think this will be expensive. The decorator talked about how good furniture was an investment, and anytime anybody says that something is an investment, what they mean is, it will cost you a ton of money.

I think I'd better postpone my plans for a new motorcycle.

Suicide of a Mule

The scene was the Superior Court of Lee County.

There stood Lonnie Roberts, a tenant farmer. His mule was dead, and he was not happy about it.

Roberts said that what happened was, his mule ran into an electric fence on the property of his neighbor, Lacy Oldham, and was electrocuted. The problem, said Roberts, was that Oldham had hooked the electric fence up to a Carolina Power & Light Co. 110-volt line, instead of a little battery, and the resulting jolt had not merely stung his mule but had zapped him to mule heaven.

It was a good mule, and Roberts wanted $500 for it. So he sued both Oldham and CP&L. It happened in 1946.

CP&L officials had one thing going for them. They had A.Y. Arledge as their attorney. The response he filed to the lawsuit is the funniest thing ever written about a mule.

"It is a matter of common knowledge amongst those acquainted with mules that a mule is endowed with a genius for self-preservation," wrote Arledge. "He will skirt the brink of a cliff or a ditch bank with the care and surefootedness of a goat, but in the case of a horse the driver must intervene to prevent him from going over.

"In the matter of discovering and avoiding hidden dangers it is common knowledge that a mule has an intelligence far superior to that of man. It enables him to know when there is an unsound sill under a bridge without his having to look under it. It is well known that he can tell when a bog is miry or when there is quicksand in a stream. It is well known that he can detect the presence of a snake hidden in the grass, whether it is in the form of a human being who proposes to do him danger or whether it be a serpent vainly lying in wait for an opportunity to sink its fangs in his wily hocks. A snake-bitten mule is rarely if ever known.

"There are many other instances far too numerous to recount in which the melancholy and poker-faced mule can sense situations and foresee consequences which may prove adverse to his personal well being.

"It has been adjudged that electricity on a wire is a danger hidden to man because it gives no warning of its deadly presence. Vision cannot detect it. It is without color, motion or body, and being odorless, the only means of its discovery lies in the sense of touch. However, the genius of a mule enables him to discover the presence of electricity on a wire fence without resorting to his sense of touch."

Arledge then set out to prove that the whole affair was the fault of the mule itself and certainly not the fault of the power company.

"It is a matter of common knowledge that a mule is a hybrid, a strange creature never intended and apparently unwelcome by Nature, so much so that he is denied the power to propagate his own kind. Except for a slip in Nature's law, his like would not exist at all.

"When the bridle is on, he is convinced that he is under his master's restraint, and the quality of the horse family dominates him. He acts with dependable obedience, commonly called horse sense. But once the bridle is off, the quality of the ass asserts itself and he displays the vicious attitude commonly called jackassery, and those who know him best, trust him least. The result is that in the former case he may be expected to act like an ass's horse and in the latter like a horse's ass, for indeed he is both.

"Being carelessly allowed to run at large and to thus disport himself in his likeness of an ass, as mules are wont to do in such circumstances, said mule knew of the presence of the deadly current. The deceased mule, in reckless disregard for his own safety did heedlessly run against said wire fence and became his own malefactor."

In other words, said Arledge, the mule committed suicide, and no one, especially CP&L, should have to pay a dime.

J.A. Weeks of Garner, who for many years was an attorney for CP&L, provided me a copy of the lawsuit. He said the suit eventually had been dismissed.

CP&L spokesman Mac Harris — who knows a lot about electric fences, having been a country boy himself, and who is still seen to wear cowboy boots with his three-piece suit — says the lawsuit was indeed filed and was most likely dismissed.

The Ghastly Beast of Bladenboro

Bladenboro

Woody Fussell can't help but smile when he remembers the Beast of Bladenboro.

You might say Fussell invented the Beast, made a nice piece of change on it and then killed it off, all the while not knowing if there even was such a thing.

For 10 days in January 1954, the eyes of the thrill-seeking world were on the little Bladen County town. Something dark and evil from the swamp was loose, and blood was being spilled. It was great fun.

"I was the mayor then and Roy Fores, the chief of police, came to me and reported that for three straight days a dog had been killed and that it looked like all the blood had been sucked out of them," Fussell said last week. "I had been calling in news items to the Wilmington paper, so I called them with the story. A little publicity never hurt a little town."

No one raised the question of how one could tell if a dead dog was bloodless, but nevertheless, the next day the paper gleefully told the world in a front-page story that a "mystery killer beast with a vampire lust" was at large in Bladenboro.

Things got real crazy real fast.

Hunters from all over the state poured into Bladenboro, armed to the teeth with all manner of firearms. The merely curious came to gawk and maybe catch a glimpse. Tourists made detours off U.S. 301 to come to Bloody Bladenboro. The news spread across the nation on the wire services, and reporters came running.

There were wonderfully juicy tales to report to an eager audience. Not a one of them was confirmed.

Most of the reports were along the lines of: "Goodness gracious, why, just over yonder some ugly thing come up out of the woods and grabbed my dog and drug him off in the woods and drank all his blood."

Fussell said: "Every farmer who had a dog or a hog die during that time said the Beast got it. Actually, I never saw anything."

The drama drew Bladenboro's nerves as tight as the E-string on a mail-order guitar.

"Folks were afraid to go out of their houses at night," Fussell said. "Some of them were afraid of the Beast, and some of them were afraid of the hunters. The woods were full of hunters."

One night, a mob of more than 500 men, most of them armed, gathered near Bladenboro's mill village section after a woman reported that she had almost been attacked in her very own back yard by the Beast. The mob had come to get that swamp devil. Or maybe just to get drunk, shoot some guns and have a little fun.

"That was the night I considered calling the governor and asking for the National Guard," Fussell said. "Not to get the monster but to control that mob. We already had sheriff's deputies and the highway patrol here."

Fussell, who operated the town's one movie theater, saw a chance to make a buck on the Beast. At the peak of the hysteria, he went to Charlotte and rented an old B-movie called "The Big Cat" and stuck up posters advertising it around town. The movie was a sellout.

But all good things must end, and so did the Beast.

"It got to the point it was very, very dangerous," Fussell said. "I was afraid somebody was going to get killed, and I figured if there had been anything in the swamp, one of those hunters would have found it."

A local resident "had shot a bobcat, and I had him bring it to town. We hung it up and I announced that it was the Beast and it had been killed. I took a picture of it and sent it to the newspapers.

"It died out after that."

Was there ever a real Beast?

"I don't think so," Fussell said. "I think it was about 10 percent real and 90 percent imagination. It might have been a pack of wild dogs that got those first three dogs. I never saw a beast or any of the animals that it was supposed to have killed."

I asked the former mayor, just between us, if there was a

chance the whole thing was his brainchild, a harmless publicity stunt?

"No, the chief did report those first three dogs," he said, with a grin and a twinkle. "But I may have pulled it along a little after it got started."

Tall Tales From the Highlands

Fannie MacLendon was dying.

There was nothing anyone could do for her. Her fever was raging, and the pregnant wife of John MacLendon did not seem long for this world.

There were no doctors available in those days, the days of the early 1700s when the lands along the upper Cape Fear River were being settled by the Highlanders of Scotland.

A neighbor named Rosa MacGill, a woman experienced in the art of herbal medicine, came to see whether she could help poor Fannie. She made poultices and brewed herbal teas from plants she had gathered along the river and along nearby Buckhorn Creek.

But Rosa was too late. Fannie had slipped into a coma, and a little while later, she died.

John buried his wife in the cemetery of Barbecue Church, a Presbyterian church that still stands in western Harnett County. It was the gathering place — the spiritual heart — of the early Scottish community.

An Englishman attending Fannie's funeral noticed that she was to be buried wearing a beautiful ring.

Night fell. The Englishman crept into the cemetery of Barbecue Church and made his way to the fresh grave that held Fannie's body. He scooped out the soft, damp earth and uncovered her coffin.

He opened the coffin and reached for Fannie's hand, the hand that wore the beautiful ring. He reached for his knife to cut off the finger that wore the ring, the ring he wanted so much that he was willing to rob a grave to get it.

Fannie opened her eyes and looked into the grave robber's face.

The Englishman screamed and leaped to his feet. He ran screaming through the cemetery, thinking, I am sure, that the very Hounds of Hell were on his heels.

He did not see the open grave that had been dug for a man

named John MacRea, who was to be buried the following day.

He fell into MacRea's grave and sprained his ankle so badly that he was unable to get out until the next day when pallbearers brought MacRea to his final resting place.

In the meantime, Fannie, who had only been in a fever-induced stupor and was not really dead, apparently had been revived by the cool night air that poured into her open coffin as the grave robber did his dirty work.

Although weak, she managed to make her way out of the grave and walk home. When she arrived, her husband opened the door, and there before his eyes, with the dirt of the graveyard still on her burial dress, stood his beloved Fannie.

He was surprised.

He slammed the door in his wife's face and almost fainted. But then he came to his senses and opened the door again and welcomed his wife home.

A week later, Rosa was called again to the MacLendon home, where she assisted in the birth of Little John MacLendon. Mother and baby did just fine.

Robber Gets the Last Laugh

Sometimes you just can't help but pull for the bad guys.

There was a bank robber loose in the land. He was real good at his work and made off with thousands of dollars from various banks. Finally his luck ran out and the robber was caught, tried, convicted and sent to prison. He got one last chance to say a tearful farewell to his loving wife and three little children before going to prison to pull a long sentence.

But while the authorities had caught the robber, they had not recovered the money he had stolen, and it was a considerable sum.

They did everything they could think of to make the fellow tell them what he had done with all that money. But he kept quiet, never giving even a hint as to what he had done with the loot. He wouldn't even admit he'd had it.

The authorities badgered and cajoled him all that first winter in prison, but he wouldn't break.

Finally it came to be spring and the robber wrote a letter to his poor wife back home. The authorities, figuring he might try to tell his wife what he'd done with all the money, were intercepting all of his mail before it left the prison.

One early spring day, they opened one of his letters to his wife and read the following: "And honey, whatever you do, don't dig or plow in the garden this year. Skip a garden this year."

Well, that was all it took. The authorities swooped down on that little patch of ground like locusts. They went to work digging with all manner of implements. They shoveled and they hoed. They turned that plot of ground over time after time. They broke up clods of dirt. They dug down 2 feet, raking every piece of dirt to find a clue. They just knew they had the old bank robber this time and were even laughing at him for being so dumb as to write that letter telling where the money was.

But they didn't find a thing. They dug in that half-acre garden plot for two days and left with nothing to show for their efforts but blisters and a thoroughly broken-up plot of ground.

The next day the robber wrote another letter to his wife: "Now, Honey, you can go ahead and plant the garden."

The Miraculous Mule Cure

An old farmer was making his way along a dirt road. He was riding in a wagon that was being pulled by his two mules, Blue and Jack.

It was a peaceful, idyllic scene until the farmer rounded a curve and over the hill came a speeding dump truck. The truck driver, going way too fast, slammed into the wagon, the farmer and the mules and sent them flying in all directions. The two mules ended up severely injured, the wagon was destroyed and the farmer was thrown into the ditch.

The farmer sued the truck company for damages and, on the day of the trial, he showed up in court with more bandages than an Egyptian mummy.

The defense attorney started questioning the old farmer about his injuries: "How is it, sir, that you come in here all hurt up when it is a well-documented fact that you plainly said at the wreck that you were not hurt? Several people heard you say then that you were fine. How can you explain that, sir?"

The old farmer shifted painfully in his courtroom seat and said, "It is simple, sir. One of the first people at the wreck was the sheriff. He went over and looked at my old mule Blue. He asked what was wrong with him and somebody told him that Blue had a broken back. So the sheriff whipped out his pistol and shot Blue right in the head to put him out of his misery.

"Then he walked over to my old mule Jack and asked what was wrong with him. Somebody told him both of Jack's back legs were broken, so the sheriff whipped out his pistol again and shot Jack right in the head to put him out of his misery.

"Then the sheriff came over to where I was lying in the ditch. He asked what was wrong with me. I couldn't move a muscle or a bone, but I sure told him I was just fine."

The Rev. Cleve Wilkie of Kinston, a retired Baptist minister and my favorite storyteller, told me those stories. I hope you enjoyed them.

The Man Who Ran Like a Horse

Newport

This is the Legend of Trotting Jim, the man who thought he was a horse.

Trotting Jim was not his real name, of course. He was Louis Wiggins, a Lenoir County man who moved to Carteret County after the Civil War and became a postman.

He got his colorful name because he ran his entire rural mail route, a lengthy route that ran from Newport to Swansboro to Beaufort and then back home to Newport. Those were the olden days before the turn of the century, and Trotting Jim ran because a mere horse couldn't have made it through the woods, over the fields and across the creeks, in good weather and bad.

It was more than his amazing ability to run that got him the name of Trotting Jim. Some say Jim actually thought he was a horse because he sure acted like one sometimes. He was known to bray and buck before he started his route and even to harness himself to a small mail-wagon when there was more than he could carry on his strong back. The part about whipping himself with a crop might be an exaggeration.

He probably knew he wasn't really a horse but he had great fun pretending to be one. The legend goes that on Sundays, after running with the mail all week, Jim would harness himself to the family buggy and take his wife and six children for a ride. One time, they say, he even bolted and ran away, leaving his wife and children in the dust. Neither history nor legend recalls what Mrs. Trotting Jim had to say when he got home, but you probably wouldn't have wanted to be there.

Country folks are polite, so it was natural that Jim would be invited to share meals with the folks he served on his route. Jim was a fun-loving fellow, and on one occasion he caused a woman to become practically hysterical when he ran into the front yard, snorting and braying like a horse, and then fell into the yard and rolled in the dust. They say the woman ran screaming from her kitchen.

He could really run, long and fast. They tell the tale in these parts that one day Jim and his family took a flock of sheep to New Bern. Jim put his family on the train back to Newport, waved goodbye as the train pulled out and then took off running for home. They say he met them at the Newport station when the train arrived.

But the greatest Trotting Jim story of all involved a traveling salesman who had a fine team of horses, the four-legged kind.

Trotting Jim met the salesman at the post office in Swansboro. The salesman was proud of his team and, as proud men will do, fell to bragging about how strong and fast they were. One thing led to another, and when Jim heard the man say he was heading to Newport, Jim bet him that he could outrun his fine team of horses. The bet was five dollars and the finish line would be the Newport post office.

The salesman thought ·it was all very funny, and when he pulled into the Newport post office and did not see Jim there, he said, smiling all the while: "Say, has anybody here seen a crazy man who thinks he can outrun a horse?"

"Yup," he was told, "Jim's been here. He waited for you about 30 minutes but he said he had to move on to Beaufort." The salesman left the five dollars for Jim.

Jim carried the mail, running barefoot, for 20 years, but then more and better trains came along and they didn't need a man of his particular skill anymore. But he was always there when you needed him. He'd run for the doctor and be back before the doctor arrived.

Some people thought Trotting Jim was a crazy man, and some people were afraid of him. They would back off when he came running into town, snorting and acting like a horse. But they respected him for his ability with real horses. They say he had a way with them and, some say, he could even talk to them in a language they could understand.

No one knows how much of this is true, of course. Jim died many years ago at the age of 75, and the legends about him have grown over the years. But one thing is certain, Trotting Jim could haul the mail.

He Drowned But Lived to Tell

Rocky Mount

Vernon Draughon is a 33-year veteran detective with the Rocky Mount Police Department. So when he tells you a story is true, you can take it to the bank.

The events in this story took place 20 years ago in Rocky Mount.

"Jack and Jim were toothbrush buddies," he said. "They painted houses together, fished together and drank out of the same bottle. In their social circle, it was better to French kiss a jackhammer than to tangle with them.

"One spring day they were painting a house on Falls Road near the Tar River. Finishing early in the afternoon, they wrapped their brushes, put them in oil and drove to the Airport Tavern."

The boys had a few beers and decided to go fishing. They had their gear in the trunk of the car, so after picking up some worms and crickets, they were ready.

"Before leaving, they bought two six-packs of beer and then went to the ABC store and bought a bottle of liquor to use as yodeling oil," Vernon said. "Then they headed straight for the river."

The boys had continued to drink, so by the time they reached the river they were, as Vernon puts it, "walking lightly and feeling no pain."

There were several boats tied up along the river. While Jim unloaded their gear, Jack ran down to the riverbank and jumped in one of them. He started running bank and forth until he slipped.

The boat was tied to a trailer hitch that was driven into the riverbank, with the rope tied around a steel ball. Jack came down face first and hit his head on the steel ball.

"He went under the water, came up and gave a faint cry and went back under," Vernon said. "Jim ran down to the river and saw Jack lying face down in the water. He pulled and tugged and finally got him out of the water and on the bank. He applied what first aid he knew, but Jack wouldn't respond.

"Jim jumped in his car and drove to the fire station about a mile away. The firemen sent a truck and notified the rescue unit to meet them at the river."

It was all to no avail. Jack was a goner. The coroner, who also was a doctor, came and pronounced him dead. They placed his still-dripping body in the ambulance and slowly drove to the funeral home.

"When the ambulance arrived at the funeral parlor, only the bookkeeper and custodian were on duty," Vernon said. "The other people had gone to Enfield to pick up a body. Jack was placed on a marble slab in the 'slumber room,' and the door was closed.

"Jack's employer was contacted and relayed the sad news to the work crews coming in. They were saddened to hear of his fate. A flower collection was taken, and pallbearers were selected.

"Meanwhile, back at the funeral parlor, all was quiet except for the piped-in music.

"Suddenly, as if a volcano was erupting, a hot stream of muddy water spewed out of Jack's mouth. He sat up on the slab. Still belching and heaving, he staggered out of the slumber room into the hall. He saw the custodian and said, 'Where am I?' The custodian never answered but made a quick exit out the front door.

"Jack continued down the hall, hitting both walls as he went. The bookkeeper was startled but not alarmed. He asked for a cigarette, and she gave him one and called the rescue squad. They came and took him to the hospital."

And who should be on duty in the hospital emergency room but the doctor who had pronounced Jack dead.

"The doctor was appalled to see Jack but maintained his professional dignity. He tried to explain to him what had happened, but what Jack knew in medical language could be put on a postage stamp. All he could understand was that he had so much fluid in his body that the doctor couldn't detect a pulse.

"Jack left the emergency room, went home and took a drink.

His nerves were all to pieces.

"Soon thereafter both men quit drinking, joined the church and set their faces clean and shining to serve their Lord."

A Killing and a Lynch Mob

Bogue

Elijah Weeks missed breakfast at the widow Julia Taylor's house that June morning. He was a 56-year-old bachelor, and it was his custom to join the Taylor family for his meals.

No one knew it yet, but Weeks was dead, his body in his bedroom over the small community store he ran.

It was a death that angered and frightened the people of the mainland community of Bogue and the people of Salter Path out on the Banks. They had known Weeks well, and his violent death meant that a killer was in their midst.

Their fear and their anger led to one of the most brutal executions ever in Eastern North Carolina. It would be a public lynching.

And it also would become one of the wonderful stories Lillian Golden told Kay Stephens. They are recorded in Kay's book, "Judgment Land: The Story of Salter Path."

As Lillian tells it, three men found Weeks' body. He was on his knees by the side of his bed. A sheet was draped over his head. The men removed the sheet and found a rope around Weeks' neck. He had been strangled.

The discovery sent a shock wave through the isolated communities. It was 1899, and people were on their own.

The sheriff sent two men to investigate the murder. They found footprints leading from the store to the sandy road that led to the east. A man told the deputies he had seen a stranger in the area the night before.

There was a stranger living in the neighborhood. His name was Patrick, and he immediately became the prime suspect. The deputies went to find him, but he was not at home. They went back to the store and began to follow the tracks in the soft sandy road.

The trail led them near Newport, where they found the remains of a camp fire and the skin of a cured ham. The deputies talked to people who reported seeing a stranger matching Patrick's description heading toward New Bern. The killer was on the run.

Afraid that Patrick would try to flee by boat, the deputies hurried to the New Bern docks, where they found him on board the steamer Neuse. He was wearing new shoes from Weeks' store, and in his baggage they found other goods stolen from the store. Patrick was arrested and was taken to the Beaufort jail to await trial.

But it was not over for the people of Salter Path and Bogue. They were angry that one of their own could be so brutally killed. They wanted revenge. They wanted to kill Patrick.

Several days after the arrest, a group of 12 men, led by one of the community leaders, met on Pettiford Creek and sailed into the night on a coastal sharpie, a traditional sailboat. Just before they landed in Beaufort, they blackened their faces. They went to the jail, took the keys away from the jailer and took Patrick.

They sailed for Salter Path and ran into a storm. They tied Patrick to the anchor so that if the boat went down, he would surely go with it.

The county sheriff and two deputies took off after the mob in a steam-powered boat. But the mob would not surrender and fired a warning shot at the sheriff. The sheriff backed off and let them go, making no other effort to stop them.

They landed at dawn at Sanders Point. Patrick was taken inland, where he was questioned roughly all day. Finally, he confessed to the murder.

The next night the mob returned and offered Patrick food. He was too frightened to eat. His fear was well-founded.

The mob took him to a large live oak tree, where they tied him with a rope like the one that had been used to kill Weeks. Twelve men loaded their rifles. Patrick began to scream and curse and cry. His wails could be heard throughout the community. Many women and children gathered to watch what was going to happen.

The leader of the mob, one of the most prosperous men in the community, told the gunmen, "Now if any of you fail to shoot when I give the signal, I'll shoot you myself." He then turned to Patrick and said, "Now, you scoundrel, we're going to give you some of what you gave Elijah."

They all fired at once, and Patrick's body was riddled.

The men who killed Patrick were never caught, although everyone in the community knew who they were.

The Great Car Washout

East Bend

Old-time story-tellers are getting hard to find. But the tradition lives in Ed Phillips of the East Bend community near Winston-Salem in Yadkin County:

"It was on a Saturday morning in June 1947. My daddy decided him and us young'uns would wash the Chevy.

"Since we did not have running water back then, the only choice was the branch below the hog lot. Daddy had us get up all the stuff to wash the car, which consisted of two peck buckets, some rags, lye soap, a bush ax and a shotgun. The bush ax was for cutting the bushes down so that we could get the car to the branch. The shotgun was for snakes.

"While my daddy took a screw-driver and pried the dried mud from around the gas pedal, us young'uns took whisk brooms and started cleaning the seats. The front seats were not hard, but the backseat was a dilly. Daddy had Walker fox hounds, and he could not get them all in the trunk. The dogs he could not get in the trunk naturally went in the backseat. We could sweep a lot of the hairs out, but a lot of them stuck in the seat cover.

"Next, we wet our rags in the branch and went to wiping the interior down. I thought wiping down the interior was crazy 'cause all we were doing was creating a thin mud film on the seats that would ruin our hand-me-down Sunday suits.

"The next thing we did was dip up branch water in the buckets and mix up the lye soap in them. I suspected we had the mixture a little strong when the minnows and crayfish floated to the top as dead as a doornail. I knew for sure something was wrong when we rinsed the car off and the maroon paint was a dull red.

"Daddy didn't comment on the paint because he was staring intently at the windshield and side glasses, which had been tinted by the lye soap. Daddy got in the car and said he could see out the windshield OK, but everything looked kind of blue.

"Daddy said he would take the clean old Chevy back to the house. Well, sir, the Chevy would not hit a lick because we had drowned out the motor. Daddy ground on the starter till he ran the battery down. That was when Daddy blew his top.

"He ordered my older brothers to run to the house and get the battery that was hooked up to our old battery radio and us little young'uns to get some dry rags to dry the ignition wires.

"When we got back down to the branch, the top of the car was covered with wet, greasy ignition wires. After a lot of fussing and fuming, the old Chevy finally fired up.

"We knew Daddy was really mad when he left. He was doing real good till he came to the hog lot. The road took a sharp left turn at the hog lot, and that is where the Chevy lost traction and plowed sideways into the hog lot, which killed our shoat right out. The sow and her gang of pigs, excited by all the commotion, made a quick exit out of the hog lot.

"We stood right there and watched Daddy blow the motor up in a cloud of smoke, being he was stuck axle-deep in hog manure. Daddy told my brothers to get the mule hitched up to the car pronto, while he went to the house and cussed out Mama. The only reason I could figure for him cussing out Mama was that she must have been badgering him to wash the car.

"Daddy came stalking back down to the hog pen and tried to get the mule to pull the car out. She was hooked up in a situation like this for the first time, and she balked. My daddy gave that balked mule one of the worst beatings any of us ever witnessed. The mule could not stand but so much, so she lunged into the trace chains and jerked the car to dry ground. But in the meantime, her back hoof caught a rock and threw it through the windshield, and it landed right smack in the backseat.

"Now here is what we had by washing a little dust off the Chevy back in 1947: faded paint, tinted windshield, grease all over the top, a thin mud film on the seats that ruined our hand-me-down Sunday suits, a dead battery, a broke windshield, a smelly rock in the back seat, scratches all over the side of the car where it went through the hog lot, hog manure all up under the car, a blowed motor, a dead shoat that would have to be ground up into sausage, a hog lot to repair, a sow and bunch of pigs to run back up, a cussed-out Mama and a sore mule."

Initiation of a 'City Boy'

Mount Olive

Joe was a traveling salesman who worked the small towns of Eastern North Carolina. He was a city boy, just starting out in business, and everybody knows a salesman has got to be sociable.

It was 50 years or so ago, and business was done for the day. Joe took an after-supper stroll through town and happened on a bunch of fellows sitting around the barber shop.

Joe sat off to the side to listen to the conversation. He knew that a newcomer, especially a fellow with "city boy" written all over him, was well-advised to keep quiet until invited to join in the talking.

Finally, one of the regulars asked him a question, and soon Joe was a full-fledged member of local society. It came to closing time, and the boys adjourned to the back room to take a drink. You just never know when the preacher might happen by the front window.

The jar got passed a few times, and soon Joe was feeling warm and relaxed.

One of the fellows, Freddie, said he had been up the street that afternoon and got to talking to some pretty girls. It seems that one of them — her name was May — said she thought Joe was a fine figure of a man and she'd like to get to know him better.

Then Freddie closed in for the kill.

Suddenly Joe heard the awful sound of a window being raised and a double barrel shotgun being closed. That is one of those sounds you can recognize in the dark the first time you ever hear it, especially if there is any chance at all it is being pointed at you.

"You thought I was in Wilmington, didn't you?" yelled an angry voice. "I'm wise to you."

That was followed by the fearsome blast of a 12-gauge. Then things started happening quickly. Freddie yelled, "I'm shot, I'm shot, help me," while the boys and Joe took off across the field. More shots followed, as well as more shouts from Freddie and more curses from the outraged bootlegger.

To heck with the car and to heck with Freddie seemed to be the popular notion as Joe and his new friends flew down the railroad tracks for town.

Finally they stopped and decided to go back and get the car. They crept back and found Freddie sitting on the running board with blood all over his leg.

They got in the car and tore out of there to take Freddie to the doctor's house. They helped him inside and waited in another room. The doctor soon came back and told them that it looked bad for Freddie and that he would have to amputate.

And wouldn't you know it, just then the door opened and in walked a deputy sheriff. He had come to arrest the whole lot of them for a number of violations, like leaving the scene of a felony, possession of illegal booze, trespassing and you name it.

Joe knew his career was down the drain. But then a ray of hope shone brightly. The deputy was in the other room, and lo and behold, the window was open.

Out the window Joe went and beat it to where his car was parked. He took off leaving a rooster tail of dust behind him. He had it made until the deputy's car ran him down and forced him to stop.

They all piled out: the deputy, a suddenly very healthy Freddie, the rest of the barbershop boys and even the doctor. They were laughing so hard they couldn't hardly get their breath.

They handed the shaking young Joe the jar and said, "Joe, have a drink."

He did, because he needed it.

They did tell him that he was one of the lucky ones. Some of the fellows they had pulled that gag on had taken off running when the shotgun went off. They never did find them.

Johnny Comes Marching Home

Somewhere, a family wonders what happened to its son.

In Burgaw, they wonder whose son they have.

The crude tombstone is hand carved and faring poorly in the Pender County weather. The fading letters grow more shallow every year.

But if you brush the sand away and trace your finger along the letters, you can still make it out: "Unknown Seaman. Found on Topsail Beach. May 17, 1942."

That's all it says, and even part of that is a guess.

"He is called the unknown seaman because he came from the sea," Charles Ives of Burgaw said. "We don't know if he was a seaman. He could have been a flier. Most people think he was a British flier shot down by a submarine, but that is really just speculation. A British plane did crash about six miles from here so people assume he was British, too. It is really a lack of knowing anything else about him."

The facts are less than skimpy. On May 17, 1942, a body was found on the beach at Topsail Island near where New Topsail Beach is now. The body was taken to Burgaw, the county seat of Pender County.

There, W.P. Harrell, a funeral home operator, took charge. He placed the body in a pauper's casket and at 4 p.m. on the afternoon of May 21, 1942, the Rev. Ismael Strawbridge of the Methodist church and the Rev. P.L. Clark of the Presbyterian church conducted a graveside service for the unknown seaman. Harrell charged $50 for the casket and $4 to dig the grave. He sent the bill to the Pender County courthouse.

Some time later, a tombstone was carved by students in the Pender County Training School and placed over the grave.

Nothing happened for the next 43 years. Somewhere, perhaps, there are records of who found the body, what identification might have been on it, something to indicate who is buried there. But if the facts are there, Charles Ives cannot find them.

"It was about six weeks ago and I was walking in the cemetery late one afternoon," Ives said. "I just happened to come across the tombstone. It had sunk into the ground and all I could read was the top six inches where it said 'Unknown Seaman.' That got my interest going."

Ives found out as much of the story as is known now. Then he had an idea.

"Charles came to us and asked what we were going to do for Memorial Day," said Paul "Frenchy" Rabalais, commander of American Legion Post 165 in Burgaw. "We liked the idea from the beginning so we had a memorial service at the grave site on Memorial Day. We placed a wreath on the grave and had a memorial service.

"We don't know who he was or anything about him, but the least we can do is let the world know he had a decent burial and a service."

There is something else the veterans of the American Legion post don't know. They don't even know the nationality of the warrior they honored. For all they know, he could have been the enemy. There was a lot of German submarine activity along the North Carolina coast and several submarines were sunk or damaged. The body could have come from one of them.

"We thought about that," Rabalais said. "But it doesn't make any difference. He was a serviceman who fought for his country. We are enough of a civilized country to give him a service. We plan to hold a service there every year."

Charles Ives has a very special, very private reason for his concern for the Unknown Seaman.

"My brother Albert was a Marine, and he was killed during the invasion of Peleliu and his body was never found.

"We would appreciate it if we knew what happened to him, and somewhere, maybe even in Germany, a family is feeling the same way. At least his family would be at peace if they knew he was here."

What Charles Ives needs is information. Any scraps will do. Are there any records? Who found the body? Was it identified? What was it wearing? There are lots of questions and few answers.

All Ives knows is that the people of Burgaw have a son with no family, and a family lost a son. And Ives knows how that feels.

Remembering the Fallen

Fort Bragg

Death is a soldier's constant companion. Maybe that is why the Army handles it so well. It has had so much practice.

The 82nd Airborne Division Memorial Chapel is a building of grace and beauty. It is dedicated to the memory of fallen paratroopers whose exploits are memorialized in seven stained glass windows that fill the sanctuary with brilliant splashes of colored sunlight.

A morning sun was shining the day the young men of B Company, 2nd Battalion, 504th Infantry, marched into the chapel in their camouflage combat uniforms and highly shined boots. They doffed their red berets and sat motionless, staring at the stark scene at the front of the chapel. They had come to honor 12 soldiers who died when their helicopter crashed on a training mission.

Before them were the traditional symbols of military death. There were eight M-16 rifles with fixed bayonets standing barrel-down on a platform made for that purpose.

Sitting on each rifle butt was a helmet. And on the helmets, written in an identical hand, were the last names of the dead. They were arranged in order of rank and, within each rank, alphabetically. A pair of paratrooper boots sat in front of each rifle.

It is an old tradition. Soldiers who died in battle often were hastily buried. A weapon was jammed into the ground as a marker so that the graves could be found after the battle. The paratrooper boots are a special tradition of the airborne. The service was dignified and Army-issue. It followed an order that all 82nd memorial services would be identical. There would be no more missing-man formation flyovers for aviators, no caissons for artillerymen, no tanks for tankers.

There were two services this day, one for the eight paratroopers and another for the four crew members of Black Hawk helicopter 314. The second service was almost identical to the first. The only difference was that the aviators had flight helmets instead of combat helmets. Each service took 24 minutes. And at each service, paratroopers and fliers openly wept for their dead.

They wept for Sgt. 1st Class Robert L. Brown, the squad leader from Vale. He left a wife, Brenda. For Staff Sgt. Timothy Williams, 33, from Miami. His wife is Judy. For Spec. 5 Mike Paserba, who was only 22 and had been in the unit only one month. His wife is Mahoret. For Spec. 4 Sebastian "Sid" Correira III, who had spent all his Army time in the 82nd. He was 23, and his wife is Sandra.

Pfc. Paul Resnick was from Moorestown, N.J. He had celebrated his 19th birthday three days before he died. Pfc. Ioannis Bougas, 19, was a New York City boy who was intensely proud of his Greek heritage. Pfc. Richard Zimmerman, 21, was known to everyone in B company as "Z-Man."

And there was Spec. 4 Mackie Chism, 21, the medic. He was not an official member of the squad, but he trained with them and died with them. They called him "Doc." He was from Tiptonville, Tenn. His wife's name is Lisa.

The four fliers were from A Company, 82nd Combat Aviation Battalion. Chief Warrant Officer Arlington E. "Ollie" Ingalls, 35, was a pilot who had fought in Grenada. He was remembered for his laughter and his love of life. His wife is Dicia. Chief Warrant Officer Robert Q. "Buck" Buchanan Jr., 32, also had fought in Grenada. He was called a kind, compassionate man who loved flying more than most and was better at it than most. His wife is Sun Cha.

Sgt. Luis L. Bacallao, 23, was the crew chief. He was from Puerto Rico, and the memorial prayer was delivered in Spanish for his family. He was devoted to Black Hawk 314. His wife is Raquel. Pfc. Troy D. Pease, 19, was the door gunner. He had been in the Army only nine months, a flier for one month, and he wanted to fly with Sgt. Bacallao.

One man spoke for all who have borne arms together: "Ours was not a common friendship. It was tempered with fire, watered with tears and warmed by laughter. They will live forever on our lips and in our hearts."

A poem written by Ingalls' sister-in-law was the most fitting memorial for the 12 soldiers who died:
"We will think of you when we look toward the sky."

Recalling Life on Memorial Day

I think they would understand the way it turned out.

Memorial Day is their day, isn't it? It is supposed to be the day a grateful nation pauses to quietly thank the more than one million men and women who have died in military service to their country since the Revolutionary War.

Or is it the day the beach resorts kick into high gear for the summer season, the day the strand is covered by fish-belly white people basting themselves in coconut oil, the day the off-season rates end and the weekend you can't get in a seaside seafood restaurant with anything less than a one-hour wait.

Or is it one of the biggest shopping center sales days of the year, a day when hunting for a parking place is the prime sport for the holiday stay-at-homers.

Or is it the weekend when more people will kill themselves on the highways than any other weekend and Highway Patrol troopers work overtime picking up the pieces?

I think the men and women who died for us would understand what we do with their day. I hope they would, because if they wouldn't, if they would have insisted that it be a somber, respectful day of remembrance, then we have blown it and dishonored their sacrifice.

I knew some of those who died, and the guys I knew would have understood. They liked a sunny beach and a cold beer and a hot babe in a black bikini, too. They would have enjoyed packing the kids, the inflatable rafts, the coolers and the suntan lotion in the car and heading for the lake. They would have enjoyed staying home and cutting the grass and getting together with some friends and cooking some steaks on the grill, too.

But they didn't get the chance. They blew up in the Marine Barracks in Beirut and died in the oily waters of the Persian Gulf. They caught theirs at the airstrip in Grenada in the little war everyone laughed at. They bought the farm in the I Drang Valley and on Heartbreak Ridge and at Hue. They froze at the

Chosin Reservoir and were shot at the Pusan Perimeter. They drowned in the surf at Omaha Beach or fell in the fetid jungles of Guadalcanal. They were at the Soame and at San Juan Hill and at Gettysburg and at Cerro Gordo and at Valley Forge.

They couldn't be here with us this weekend, but I think they would understand that we don't spend the day in tears and heart-wrenching memorials. They wouldn't want that. Grief is not why they died. They died so that we could go fishing. They died so another father could hold his laughing little girl over the waves. They died so another father could toss a baseball to his son in their backyard while the charcoal is getting white. They died so another buddy could drink a beer on his day off. They died so a family could get in the station wagon and go shopping and maybe get some ice cream on the way home.

They won't mind that we have chosen their day to have our first big outdoor party of the year. But they wouldn't mind, either, if we took just a second and thought about them.

Some will think of them formally, of course. Wreaths will be laid in small, sparsely attended ceremonies in military cemeteries and at monuments at state capitols and in small town squares. Flags will fly over the graves, patriotic words will be spoken and the few people there probably will feel a little anger that no more people showed up. They'll think no one else remembers.

But we do remember. We remember Carlton and Chico and Davey and the guys who died. We remember the deal we made: If we buy it, we said, drink a beer for me.

I'll do it for you, guys. I'll drink that beer for you today, and I'll sit on that beach for you, and I'll check out the girls for you and, just briefly, I'll think of you. I won't let your memory spoil the trip, but you'll be on that sunny beach with me today.

I will not mourn your deaths this Memorial Day, my friends. Rather, I'll celebrate the life you gave me.

This Bud's for you.

Remembering Beirut's Victims

Jacksonville
The old Marine and the young Marine sat together, staring into the flickering candlelight.

The black woods outside the circle of soft yellow light were wet from three days of rain. Water dripped from the trees and turned footprints into puddles in the soft gray sand.

It was 4 o'clock in the morning. No one spoke.

They had come together to light a candle in the rain. They had come to honor fallen comrades.

Two years before, in the early hours of a bloody Beirut morning, 241 Marines had died when a young zealot drove a truck loaded with explosives into the first floor of their headquarters. In the time it takes to cough, the building was blown apart.

It had been raining in Jacksonville on that day, too.

"It has rained every time we've had a service," Doris Downs said. "We had made arrangements to move the vigil to the Presbyterian Church, but they talked us out of it. They wanted it here in the rain."

Mrs. Downs is one of the organizers of an effort to build a memorial to those fallen Marines, most of whom were stationed at Camp Lejeune. The drive to raise $180,000 needed to build the memorial has fallen on hard times as the national rage and sympathy has faded.

The vigil last week was an attempt by the Jacksonville Beautification and Appearance Commission to rekindle interest in, and donations for, the Beirut Memorial Park. They have $98,000 in the bank, a 4½-acre site donated by Camp Lejeune and a donated load of bricks.

The vigil began with a few hundred people huddled in a pouring rain on Tuesday afternoon. Appropriate words were spoken and then the long, wet night of remembering began.

They built a shrine of sorts in a clearing. There was a rustic altar made of olive drab sandbags covered by a camouflage cloth. In front of the altar was a wreath of red, white and blue carnations, festooned by a red, white and blue ribbon. The altar hid a tank of propane gas that fueled a flame that burned through the night.

Around the flame were candles that burned down to create a mound of melted wax. Most of the candles were white, but from somewhere a red candle had been burned, adding streaks of red in the ring of white. It was hard not to think of blood.

Throughout the night, people had come to the clearing to sit quietly under the funeral home tent that had been erected over the makeshift shrine. It was a place where no one asked questions.

"We had people here all night," Mrs. Downs said. "The veterans organizations and our commission had people here on two-hour shifts. There were some family members and friends here all night long."

They came alone and in groups of two and three. Some sat quietly for a few minutes and then left. Others merely walked up, gazed at the candles and turned away.

It was an easy visit for the curious, but an often hard one for the troubled. Those who felt touched by a bomb two years and half a world away found it difficult not to weep.

A tall Marine colonel stood at attention by the little flames. He stared until tears streaked his face. He saluted, turned smartly and walked away. His place was taken by a young Marine with tattoos on his forearms who pulled a candle from his pocket, knelt and lighted it from the gas flame and added it to the ring. Then he, too, faded into the darkness.

At 6 a.m., as the traffic of other Marines on their way to work on nearby Lejeune Boulevard began to build, people gathered for the final ceremony. The ring of candles was extinguished, leaving only the single flame to light the clearing for a moment.

A prayer was offered and a poem was read in the harsh, intruding lights of television cameras that had shattered the darkness. The lights swept the small gathering in the damp woods, focusing on a crying mother and then on a weeping young widow. Finally, they let them grieve in darkness.

At 6:23 a.m., the moment that 241 Marines had died in Beirut, a lone Marine bugler began the mournful melody of "Taps" as the flame slowly died.

The last lingering note faded as the flame went out. A hundred people were left standing in dark stillness, listening to the sound of broken hearts and shattered dreams.

End of a Path Paved With Tears

They sat on the floor, leaning back against the motel wall with their forearms resting on their knees.

The journey to this time and place of redemption had been long and sometimes painful. Tears had been shed, and friends had died. Women had been kissed, and babies had been held in their strong arms. Ghosts had haunted them, and memories too private to share had lived in their hearts for a long time.

But now, at 2 o'clock on a Sunday morning and just a little bit drunk, they felt a joyous peace and they drank a toast to the absent companions of their youth.

"To us, and all those like us," said a former sailor named Tony Bruce. Glasses were lifted, and the men and women of Vietnam drank deeply of good bourbon and the sweet wine of homecoming.

Two men stood by each other, once strangers but now brothers. "Welcome home, brother," one said to the other, and they embraced warmly.

For many, it was a time to say thank you to the veterans of Vietnam. They came to the memorial by the thousands on a hot Saturday afternoon to hear speeches and watch the flags wave in the spring sunshine. The speeches were what you would expect at a memorial's unveiling. There was the political rhetoric of bravado that drew cheers and quiet, deeply felt words of welcome home and official thanks for a nasty job well done.

It was a time for everyone to think about Vietnam and to think about the young men and women — really just boys and girls — they had sent off to that once-beautiful land. Some they sent to fight and some to type and some to fix airplanes and some to nurse the wounded and some to cook and some to dig latrines and some to die and some to load their dead bodies into bags to be sent home to their parents and wives and children.

But for those who came home alive, it was more than a Saturday in the sunshine. It was their time of reunion, their time to be proud, to be with people who needed no explanations and demanded nothing, to be with the brothers and sisters who understood and who really cared about them. It was their day to stand tall.

The speeches at Union Square were just fine, and the music was nice. Hundreds of thousands of dollars had been spent to make both the memorial and the dedication ceremony perfect, and it was.

But one little family did more than all the politicians and organizers ever could. They stood on the north side of the square and didn't say a word. They just held a big homemade sign that read: "Thank you for fighting."

It was the first time anyone had said that to them, and every man and woman of Vietnam who was there that day saw it, and they were touched by its heartfelt eloquence.

It was the private time that meant the most to the veterans.

The public saw them, dressed in bits and pieces of old uniforms, as they lit candles for the missing on Friday and Saturday nights and as they gathered in the square on Saturday afternoon for the dedication.

But they didn't see them in the hotel as they talked quietly and shared memories. They didn't see them on Saturday evening when the nurses gathered for dinner and suddenly found their table surrounded by the men they had kept alive after the bullets had torn into them. It was no big deal, just a group of men with drinks in their hands, standing around a table full of women cracking jokes, but it was their way of showing respect.

Respect. That is what the whole weekend was about. Respect long denied and respect long overdue. Respect they had not gotten from the one side that had chastised them for taking part in that war, and respect they had not gotten from the other side that chastised them for not winning it, whatever winning means.

But now they had it. Now they had come together. Now they had grabbed a comrade's hand and felt the bond of brotherhood that set them apart, then and now. Now they could cry with a buddy's arms around them and now they could laugh and now they could drink, and those who were there will never forget it.

In the early morning darkness of the Capitol grounds, after the music and words of glory had been swept away by the spring breezes, and after all the others had left, they came alone and in small groups to pay their private respects to their memorial and to what it meant. They stood for a moment in silence, most of them with tears in eyes that had seen too much too soon, and then they left to go home, feeling better for having been a part of it all.

"To us, and all those like us," they said.

A Place of Peace and Healing

Washington

Nothing can prepare you for the silent eloquence of The Wall.

Vietnam veterans quietly tell each other to visit it. They say that the visit will heal rather than hurt. They say it will make you feel better. And they are right.

But they cannot prepare you for its power. They cannot tell you how deeply it will touch your heart to walk the sidewalk before the 493 feet, 6 inches of polished black granite slabs bearing the names of 58,022 who died in Vietnam, Cambodia and Laos.

The Vietnam Veterans Memorial is a place of peace born in war, a place where men who were once young warriors can come and openly weep for absent companions and not feel ashamed of the tears. It is a place where one veteran will grasp another's hand and say, "Welcome home, brother," and both will feel the warm, unspoken bond that has reunited a battered generation of American veterans now heading for middle age.

The memorial was built by veterans as a gift to the American people. Veterans raised the $7 million, and that seems right. They had survived their generation's battlefields, and they had survived homecomings that for many were cold and even hostile.

But veterans came together in their rage and anguish and built far more than just another war memorial in a city dotted with stone monuments to national glory. Veterans may have given the monument to the people of America, but they built it for themselves and it remains theirs.

The Wall has become a touchstone of our generation, the place where Vietnam veterans can come and walk with the pride and dignity they have been denied.

They come by day and night, some to touch the engraved name of a friend, some to leave a private talisman, some to sit under the trees on the gentle slope and look at it and try to remember and try to forget.

The Wall was crowded on this Veterans Day, but it was a silent, respectful gathering. Thousands of Vietnam veterans, many in faded, rag-tag parts of old uniforms, stood in quiet groups while others knelt by the V-shaped wall in private reflection. They reached out a hand to touch a beloved name, to remember a friend who gave his life to save theirs, to remember a war day when they could have died but didn't. They tried to understand why. Some wept in the bright sunshine.

Some walked through the crowd looking for familiar unit insignias to ask if anyone knew what had happened to an old friend from that unit. Others had lists of names and pictures from unit yearbooks, checking their list to see how many names they could find on The Wall. Some were lucky and did not find their friends listed. Others found far too many.

There were many embraces in this place, where manly notions of private strength are set aside. Veterans reached out to the only people who would really understand, to the other men who had shared the days of their youth and nights of their terror.

Many did not come alone. They brought their wives and sweethearts and children, many of whom seemed sometimes baffled by the intense emotion The Wall released. They held tight to their men and gave them what they could. Many of them are used to it by now, for they have fought the private war with their veterans.

It is not a lifeless wall of cold, chiseled stone. To stand in front of all those faceless, dead names with no hometowns, no ages, no ranks, no branch of service and to see your face refected in the stone with them is to become a part of who they were and what they gave.

It has become a place to leave small gifts. Many bring flowers; others leave notes that tell of gratitude for lives well lived, for lives saved and for lives remembered. Some removed unit patches or decorations for valor from their old uniforms and left them by The Wall. And everywhere, along the entire length of The Wall, were small American flags.

The Wall has become more than anyone ever intended and more than anyone could have ever hoped.

It is a place for those who were part of the war and for those who care about them to come and free the pain and to be cleansed of it for a time.

For the Vietnam veterans who survived the war, The Wall is their reward to themselves.

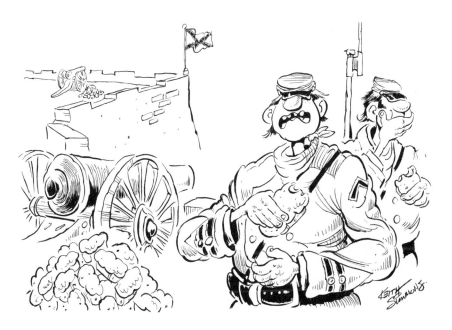

The Biscuit War

The Bread Mutiny started out as a disagreement about who could bake the best bread, but by the time it was over, the antagonists were talking about shooting each other and throwing people in jail.

The spat proved one thing: Southern boys take their biscuits seriously.

The scene is Fort Macon on North Carolina's Bogue Banks, just five miles east of Atlantic Beach. The time is 1862.

The situation for the approximately 440 Confederate soldiers inside the brick fort was deadly serious. They were surrounded by thousands of federal troops who were determined to capture the fort that protected the Beaufort-Morehead City harbor. The men inside the fort were just as determined that the fort would not fall.

The Battle of the Biscuits, however, was not a battle between North and South. It was a battle between a strong-willed

Confederate colonel from Mississippi and an equally stubborn garrison of hungry soldiers from Carteret, Craven, Wayne, Wilson and Edgecombe counties.

There were five companies of troops in the fort, and the routine was for each company to draw a ration of flour from the commissary and then for each company to bake the bread for that day's meals.

The men thought that was just fine, but Col. Moses White thought he had a better idea. It would take less flour, he figured, if one baker baked all the bread for the entire garrison. He learned that he had a man who had been a baker before the war, Pvt. Robert Church of Wayne County. White issued the appropriate orders, and the men cheerfully went along with it. They did not know what was coming.

The fort's huge oven was cleaned out and Pvt. Church, with an assistant, went to baking. The troops, probably drawn by the smell of baking bread, gathered to await the goodies.

Church pulled the first loaves of bread from the oven, and they were just dreadful. They were unfit to eat. The troops laughed a lot and yelled for Pvt. Church to try again. He did, with the same results. The good-natured troops laughed again and suggested that the hard-as-rocks loaves of bread could be used as cannon balls.

Pvt. Church kept baking but the laughter faded. It was no longer very funny. The men wanted bread, and the stuff coming out of the fort's ovens was inedible. Murmurs of discontent were heard in the fort.

A group of officers went to Col. White and diplomatically told him that his idea of fresh baked bread was just fine but that it wasn't working out, so why didn't he call the whole thing off and give the men their flour so they could bake their own bread.

The fort's doctor even took three of the best loaves Church had baked to the colonel and told him that the bread was unfit to eat and suggested that he cancel his order.

Col. White refused. He would not give in. The units officially submitted their food ration request the next morning and asked for flour, not bread. White scratched out the word "flour" and wrote in the word "bread" and Pvt. Church kept baking his loathsome loaves.

The officers went back to Col. White. "We are surrounded by Yankees by the thousands and any time now they're going to attack us and you are destroying morale with this stupid bread order," they told him.

The officers, all local fellows, told the stiff-necked colonel that if they didn't get their flour by 9 a.m., they were going to march their troops to the commissary and take what they wanted.

Col. White said if they did that, he'd place an armed guard over the flour and would arrest them all if they tried to march on his commissary.

The officers said that was just fine with them and besides, the colonel would have a tough time finding guards he could trust among the angry, and hungry, Eastern North Carolina troops they led.

They yelled back and forth awhile and the officers stormed out, ready to carry through their threat.

They went to the troops and got their raiding parties ready. The signal to attack and capture Col. White's flour would be a single drum tapping at 9 a.m.

It was a tense time. Thousands of enemy soldiers surrounded the little fort, and inside, the Bread Mutiny was boiling.

At 8:55 a.m., five minutes before the shooting was going to start, Capt. W.C. King rushed out onto the parade ground with the news that Col. White had seen the error of his ways and had canceled his order. Flour would be issued.

The Bread Mutiny was over. Bloodshed had been averted and the troops got the bread they wanted. But in the next three days, nine Carteret County soldiers deserted for home.

On Saturday, April 25, 1862, Federal troops began shelling Fort Macon. The United States flag was raised over the defeated fort at 10:22 a.m., April 26, 1862.

The Day Raleigh Almost Burned

It was cold and raining that April morning in 1865 — weather that perfectly fit the mood of Raleigh.

On the southern edge of the city were 60,000 Union troops. There was nothing to stop them from doing what they wanted to the last Confederate state capital. Confederate troops had withdrawn, leaving Raleigh unprotected. The city held its breath.

Gen. William T. Sherman's reputation had preceded him. Columbia had been destroyed a few weeks earlier, and there were those who feared that Raleigh would meet the same blazing fate.

We came very, very close.

His last name was Walsh, and that is all we know of him. He was a lieutenant in the 11th Texas Cavalry. And, single-handedly, on the morning of April 13, 1865, he almost caused the city of Raleigh to be destroyed.

A deal had been made to save the city. As Sherman's troops approached the city from Smithfield, the state government fled westward, taking with it the last military supplies and soldiers.

Local officials sent a peace mission down what is now Old Garner Road April 12 to meet with approaching Union forces. The officials promised that the city would surrender peacefully and asked that it be protected. Union Gen. Hugh Kilpatrick agreed not to harm the city, "provided no hostile act is committed against the officers and men of this army." The officials came back to Raleigh and urged the frightened people to stay in their homes as the blue-clad troops rode into town.

Kilpatrick's cavalry rode up Smithfield Street, took a right turn on Blount Street, then a left turn on South Street to the foot of Fayetteville Street. Before it stretched the city's main thoroughfare with the historic state Capitol dead ahead.

Waiting there was former Gov. David Swain with the keys to the building. It was a dead city waiting to meet its uncertain fate. The rear guard of the last Confederate army was at that moment riding west out Hillsborough Street.

The Union soldiers rode slowly up deserted Fayetteville Street in a pouring rain. They were armed and ready.

Suddenly, from a store near the intersection of Morgan and Fayetteville streets, a patrol of Texas cavalrymen led by Lt. Walsh burst from the door. Swain saw them and rushed over to tell them the Federals were in sight. The Confederate cavalrymen leapt to their saddles and rode westward.

All of them, that is, except Walsh.

He knew it was all over. Lee had surrendered to Grant in Virginia. The Confederacy was dead. The Civil War was all but over. But not for the Texan. There would be one last battle, one man against an army.

Walsh mounted his horse, rode to the middle of the street, drew his revolver and waited until the Union troops were within 100 yards.

"Hurrah for the Southern Confederacy," be bellowed and fired six shots.

He then wheeled his horse around and thundered west on Morgan Street with the enraged Union cavalry on his heels.

He tried to make a turn on Morgan Street to head for Hillsborough Street, but his horse fell. He remounted and took off again. But at the railroad overpass on Hillsborough Street, near what is now Glenwood Avenue, he was overtaken and captured.

Walsh was brought before a furious Kilpatrick. The deal had gone sour. The promise had been broken and Raleigh was in peril.

Kilpatrick, a harsh, hot-tempered man, ordered Walsh immediately executed. He was taken to Lovejoy Grove at the corner of Bloodworth and Lane streets to be hanged. Walsh asked for five minutes to write a goodbye letter to his wife 2,000 miles away in Texas. But Kilpatrick refused, and Walsh was hanged. Kilpatrick, in a moment of compassion, ordered that the city be spared in spite of Walsh's attack. But here would be no second chance, he said.

Walsh's grave is now in the Confederate section of Raleigh's Oakwood Cemetery.

The next day Abraham Lincoln was assassinated.

Neill Fulghum, a curator at the N.C. Museum of History, said: "People don't know how close we came to suffering the same fate as Columbia and Atlanta. If Kilpatrick had been killed and with Lincoln assassinated the next day, nothing could have stopped those 60,000 federal troops from destroying Raleigh."

When War Came to Raleigh

It was early Sunday afternoon in Raleigh. It was a sunny day with the temperature in the mid-50s.

The biggest show in town was a performance of Handel's "Messiah." More than 4,000 people were in Memorial Auditorium for the performance by 234 voices.

It wasn't until they walked out of the auditorium that they learned of what was happening half a world away.

U.S forces at Pearl Harbor had been attacked, and the nation was at war. It was Dec. 7, 1941.

North Carolina reacted to the news swiftly.

In New Bern and Jacksonville, which are near Marine bases, trucks rolled through the streets picking up every Marine they could find. Leaves were canceled, and every military man in the state was ordered to report to his base for further orders.

The State Fairgrounds became a military base as hundreds of soldiers from Fort Bragg were sent to Raleigh. Armed guards were placed on railroads and bridges. Soldiers patrolled the streets to speed the flow of convoys of military vehicles passing through town. Troops patrolled water, sewer and power plants. Local merchants donated food, candy, chewing gum, soft drinks and cigarettes to soldiers.

Movie theaters across the state interrupted shows to announce that the country was at war. GIs got up and left immediately, many leaving their dates behind.

The U.S. Navy announced it would begin accepting recruits from 17 to 50 years old.

Private planes at the Raleigh airport were grounded. Ham radios were ordered off the air.

Eastern Airlines announced it would accept no air freight because of the danger of bombs from saboteurs. The airline also said it had been reporting to the FBI on every reservation made by people of Japanese ancestry.

Weldon got its first taste of war on Monday when Army troops arrived to protect bridges across the Roanoke River.

Wilmington's shipyards were taken over by troops from Camp Davis at nearby Holly Ridge and highway patrolmen closed all roads to the Dow chemical plant.

In Hendersonville, vandals hurled rocks through the window of a Main Street shop owned by a U.S. citizen of Japanese ancestry.

Volunteers in Fayetteville held a street party for Fort Bragg soldiers on the Tuesday after the attack. Estimates were that 40,000 soldiers attended, along with 20,000 civilians, and that they ate 10 tons of food.

Congressman Harold Cooley of North Carolina attempted to enlist in the Army and Navy on the Wednesday after Pearl Harbor to fulfill a campaign promise that he would enlist to fight if he ever voted to send the country to war. He was not accepted.

On Thursday, it was announced that the sale of automobile tires would be suspended.

Fort Bragg authorities asked farmers on the Friday after to remove signs and arrows from their barn roofs that pointed the way to military bases. The signs had gone up during maneuvers to help lost pilots.

On Saturday, it was announced that the Rose Bowl game between Duke and Oregon State was canceled because of the war. The game was moved to Durham. Duke lost.

Air raid wardens across the state reacted with anger when they looked at their whistles. They were stamped "made in Japan." The wardens were begged not to discard them until replacements were found. Merchants in Goldsboro ordered products made in Japan removed from their shelves. Two travelers passing through Dunn had a sign on the windshield of their car that read, "We're Filipinos — Not Japs."

Fayetteville had its first air raid and blackout drill, and things went well until a train passing through town blew its whistle three times. That also happened to be the "all-clear" signal and lights came back on much too soon.

The first week of the war saw 484 men enlist in Raleigh. The recruiting stations operated seven days a week, 24 hours a day.

On Monday, 4,565 Raleigh residents signed up for volunteer defense work. In Greenville, 10 prisoners volunteered for suicide missions and said if they survived they would come back and serve out their sentences.

North Carolina had gone to war.

The Major Who Vanished

Robert Roy Clark either committed the perfect crime or was the victim of one.

It is a North Carolina mystery that has stumped federal and state law enforcement officials for 41 years.

On St. Patrick's Day, March 17, 1944, Robert Roy Clark, a 33 year old Army major, walked out the front door of a Fayetteville Street diner in downtown Raleigh and disappeared.

Was he murdered by a criminal so cunning, or lucky, that his crime has remained undetected for 41 years? Did the quiet, former newspaper reporter choose to desert the Army, for whatever reason, and get away with it?

What about the severe headaches? Did they lead to amnesia? Is there a man alive somewhere who doesn't know who he really is?

Was it just a well-planned suicide, and the body was never

found? Or was he kidnapped for the military secrets he knew?

Clark came to North Carolina shortly after March 1, 1944, when the headquarters of the Eastern Defense Command's Southeastern Sector was moved here. He was assigned as G-2 officer, a staff job that dealt with the collection of intelligence information and the protection of secret Army information. It was a sensitive job that required a top secret security clearance.

Clark was a remarkably private man, even for an intelligence officer. The Ridgewood, N.J., native joined the New Jersey National Guard and was commissioned a second lieutenant in 1935 while he was a court reporter at the Bergen, N.J., Evening Record. He came on active duty in 1941.

He was a reporter in Bergen for 10 years, a long time to be at one job, but no one at the small paper knew him very well. People who worked with him said he was a conscientious, quiet and capable man who never discussed his personal affairs. Although he was there for a decade, he had not a single close friend at the paper.

His early life was touched by tragedy. His father committed suicide by hanging when Clark was 19. Clark found his father's body and had to cut him down. That incident plunged Clark into a long, deep depression. Eleven years later his mother died, and he was stricken by depression again.

In March 1944, Clark drove into Raleigh in his 1941 cream-colored Dodge coupe and checked into a hotel. On Sunday, March 12, 1944, Clark and a fellow officer moved into the home of John A. Park, editor and publisher of The Raleigh Times, who had agreed to rent them rooms.

It was a short and odd relationship with Park. Although Clark was a veteran newspaper reporter living in the home of a veteran newspaper publisher, he never once told Park of his own civilian newspaper past. It would seem to be a coincidence Clark would have at least mentioned to his host.

Clark was at his job for a week before he disappeared. Late that week he called acquaintances at Fort Bragg and told them he was coming down for the weekend. His scheduled afternoon off was Friday, and he was scheduled to work on Saturday morning, although he told people at Fort Bragg he would be there for the weekend.

On Wednesday of that last week, Clark had lunch with a co-worker and complained of severe headaches.

Also during that week, Clark received orders to make a two-week tour of military bases in Florida, Georgia and South

Carolina. He was scheduled to leave on Monday, March 20.

Clark left the Park home at 2051 White Oak Road in Raleigh early on that last Friday morning. He left a personal check on the dresser to pay rent for the rest of March and a note saying he would be gone for 16 days. He took most of his clothes and toilet articles with him.

He drove to his office, where he made a call to the military motor pool and arranged to have a car and driver pick him up early that next Monday morning. He worked at his desk the rest of the morning and joined a co-worker for lunch at a Fayetteville Street restaurant. He told the friend he was leaving after lunch for Fort Bragg.

Clark finished his lunch first and paid his bill. His co-worker watched him walk out the front door.

He was never seen again.

Seven months later, a Hoke County deer hunter found a shocking clue in the case.

It was Oct. 16, 1944. Robert Parks was hunting deer in dense woods about two miles from Montrose in Hoke County when his dog started sniffing at a thicket.

Parks pushed aside the branches and found olive drab Army blankets.

He lifted a blanket and found a cream-colored 1941 Dodge coupe with New Jersey license plates JY35W.

The car belonged to Clark, the missing Army major, and the discovery only deepened the mystery.

Agents from Army Intelligence, the FBI, the Army's Criminal Investigation Division, the SBI as well as local police and sheriff's departments and the Highway Patrol had tried to find Clark.

They checked rooming houses and hotels around the base. They interviewed military policemen on duty at the gates. Highway patrolmen received three bulletins a day to be on the lookout for the car and Clark, a 5-foot-9-inch, 150-pound man with dark hair and metal-rimmed glasses.

Airmen flew over the forests of Fort Bragg looking for his car, while military policemen cruised the hundreds of miles of wooded trails on the post.

There was not a clue for seven months. Then Parks found the Dodge.

Investigators rushed to Hoke County. They found the car hidden under camouflage so perfect that the Army officers said it was done by an expert. Army blankets had been stretched over the car and then covered by brush. It was invisible from the air and even when standing right next to it.

Clark's empty wallet was inside the car. They found a .22-caliber pistol wrapped inside underwear in one of three suitcases containing Clark's clothes. On the seat they found his Springfield rifle. Everything was wet and covered with mildew as if it had been there a long time.

There were no bloodstains and no signs of a struggle.

There was one other clue. A woman's small valise or handbag was found nearby.

The investigation went nationwide. Clark's insurance company sent its top private investigator to follow every lead. He found nothing. A $2,000 reward for information was offered by distant relatives. No one ever claimed it.

Army investigators checked a dead-end tip that Clark had been seen with a young woman waiting for a northbound train in Salisbury. They watched his two bank accounts, one in Raleigh with $260.30 and one in New York with $665.90. There had been no large withdrawals before his disappearance and none at all afterward.

The possibilities, police said, were:

■ He hid the car and committed suicide. He was trained in camouflage and had suffered from depression. How did he do it with the guns left in the car? Was there a gun no one knew about? Where was the body?

■ He was kidnapped by enemy spies who wanted information. That seems unlikely because his information, while classified, was hardly worth the risk involved in working so deep in an enemy country.

■ He was an enemy agent himself who had been under deep cover for years and for some reason had now left his post. His lack of friends and reluctance to talk about his past made investigators suspicious.

■ He was robbed and killed by a hitchhiker who hid the body so successfully it was never found. He had been known to pick up hitchhikers.

■ He simply went AWOL, using his intelligence skills to mask his trail. There was no indication he was unhappy, although he had expressed some desire to be in the fighting in Europe. Some investigators suspected he staged his own disappearance and enlisted in the Army again under a false identity so he could be in action.

■ It was amnesia. There had been the severe headaches, but why did he hide the car and leave the clothes behind?

On May 25, 1954, the file was closed when the Army changed Major Clark's official status from AWOL to presumed dead.

Someone had gotten away with a perfect crime.

The Saga of the Wright Brothers

Kill Devil Hills

They did not just blow into town, invent the airplane one windy morning, and sail off again.

Wilbur and Orville Wright — and if you think their names are a bit old fashioned in this age when most boys seem to be named Jason or Joshua, note that their brothers were named Reuchlin and Lorin — were precious kids who would have driven less understanding parents nuts, according to historical accounts.

Consider Orville's school attendance. The son of a bishop in the United Brethren Church, Orville would dutifully troop off to first grade each morning, freshly washed and combed, and return home each afternoon at the appointed hour.

One day, several weeks into the school term, Mrs. Wright visited the school to see how her son was doing. She was rather shocked to learn that Orville had not shown up in class since the first day. The teacher assumed the family had moved.

Orville returned home as usual that day to find a most curious mother. She soon learned that each morning he had been going to the home of another boy about his age. It seems the other boy's mother had recently purchased a new sewing machine and put her old one in the barn behind the house. Each morning the two miscreants would pretend to go to school and, instead, slip into the barn where they would spend the school day playing with the old machine and trying to figure out how it worked.

Orville was a tinkerer from birth. He was in business for himself by the time he was 9 or 10 years old. He made kites for the other boys in the neighborhood and had perfected them until their wood was so thin it would bend in the wind, not unlike the wings of the airplane he would later build.

But not all his youthful ventures were successful. Chewing tar was a popular thing for boys to do and Orville figured that if he mixed sugar with the tar and wrapped it in paper, he could sell it and turn a profit. He and another boy spent most of a day mixing tar with sugar and sampling it to see how it tasted. They were deathly ill at the end of the day and gave up on the project.

One day Orville decided to put on a wild animal circus. Dayton, Ohio, was short of wild animals so he conspired with a friend whose father was a taxidermist. They collected the stuffed animals and then set about collecting an audience. Brother Wilbur was four years older than Orville and tended to avoid his childish endeavors but did agree to write a publicity release about the circus. They slipped the notice into the post office box of the town's newspaper editor, who thought it was funny and mentioned it in his column.

Come the day of the circus, Orville and his partner rode high-wheel bicycles through the streets of Dayton with a gang of boys pulling an old wagon behind them. On the wagon was a stuffed grizzly bear. The strange procession drew a lot of customers, and the circus became highly profitable. The Wright brothers learned the advantage of publicity, and years later, after they flew at Kill Devil Hills, the first telegram they sent with the big news was to the Norfolk newspaper.

Orville and Wilbur went into the newspaper business when Orville was 15. They not only wrote the paper, they invented a press on which to print it. Wilbur had earlier had a job folding an eight-page church newspaper and, tiring of the drudgery, had invented a machine to do the folding for him.

It wasn't until Orville was 24 and Wilbur was 28 that they began seriously thinking about flight, and they were in their mid- to late 30s by the time they flew in 1903. And that venture almost ended in disaster several times.

Just getting to Kill Devil Hills the first time almost did them in. They arrived in Norfolk by train Sept. 7, 1900, and rode a boat to Elizabeth City. It took them four days to find someone to take them to the Outer Banks. Finally they found Israel Perry, a fisherman, who agreed to take them over in his flat bottom river schooner.

The Wrights didn't know that the old schooner was almost ready to fall apart from decay and the ravages of insects and weather.

A September gale caught them in the middle of Albemarle sound and ripped away the sails. Only by frantic bailing did the Wright brothers and Perry reach the shore, where they repaired the boat and finally landed, two days later, at Kitty Hawk Bay.

They made four flights in December 1903, and the popular notion is that the original plane is now at the Smithsonian Institution's Air and Space Museum in Washington.

Well, partly. Only about 40 percent of the plane is there. The rest of it was destroyed at Kill Devil Hills when the wind blew it over and wrecked it. Even the muslin fabric has been replaced.

But parts of the original fabric have flown again. On three separate occasions, pieces of the fabric have been taken into space, including the flight of Apollo 11 that landed on the moon.

Memories Outlast Bulldozers

Wilmington

She was 68 years old when they tore her down. She had faced the worst the turbulent Atlantic Ocean could throw at her, storms that had leveled everything around her for miles. But in the end, it took bulldozers to move what the hurricanes had been unable to budge.

But bulldozers can't dislodge memories and the memories of the grand Lumina ballroom live on in Wrightsville Beach. The old-timers can remember her bright lights and her smooth dance floor and the big bands that flocked to play the sweet music of their youth.

The Lumina is but a shimmering vision in a forgotten dream, a gracious relic of memory from a time of dapper gentlemen with fine, sleek ladies on their arms; of silver flasks and trolley cars; of dance cards and chaperons, of starlight on sea and sand.

The beach was a wasteland when the Lumina was built. It is hard to imagine in these days of condos and traffic jams at the beach, but there was a time when only the hardy who owned boats could get there. The beach was wild and rugged country.

Enter the Consolidated Railway, Light and Power Co. in 1905.

"They are the ones who opened the beach," said Harry Warren, a historian and researcher with the New Hanover County Museum. "They operated a trolley out to the beach, and to encourage people to ride the trolley, they built the Lumina as a place to go. It was at the end of the line."

There is nothing now that even comes close to what the Lumina was. During the day, it was a bath house where you could rent bathing suits. But at night it became the most romantic ballroom you could imagine.

The dance floor itself was 50 feet by 120 feet, 6,000 square feet of polished hardwood. There was a special band shell, scientifically designed to enhance the sound of the great orchestras that came to play. The dance floor was surrounded by another 6,000 square feet of veranda that overlooked the ocean.

There were seats for several hundred on the ocean side and they looked out at a huge movie screen that stood in the surf, where silent movies were shown every night.

And the entire building was outlined in lights. It was such a bright sight that mariners used it to navigate up and down the coast. "Lumina" means light, and she was light.

"It was one of the grandest ballrooms in the country," Warren said. "People came from all over the Southeast to dance the night away at the Lumina."

They danced to the finest orchestras. Tommy Dorsey, Cab Calloway, Paul Whiteman, Stan Kenton, Guy Lombardo, Benny Goodman and Kay Kyser all played there regularly.

"They had no trouble getting the great bands," Warren said. "They wanted to play there because it was such an elegant, high society place that had great acoustics.

"It was also very strict," he said. "A man had to be introduced to a lady before he could ask her to dance. The girls had dance cards they filled up and there was a stag line for the men. And there was no liquor allowed on the premises, but I have heard tales of men burying their flasks in the sand dunes."

The elegance of the Lumina and the society it beckoned to began to fade about the time of World War II. A bridge was built to the beach in 1940, opening it to anyone. Tens of thousands of military men were in the area and they headed for the Lumina because there was no place else to go. The luster began to fade as the lights were turned off to keep German submarines from using it as a navigation aid.

The post-war years saw the decline of the Lumina. There was rock 'n' roll music and a bar opened and the gracious grande dame of the beach became a pavilion with pinball machines.

"But even at the end, during its worst days, the building maintained a class and style you don't see any more," Warren said. "It never fell apart. The mystery and elegance still came through.

"The imagination was fueled when you walked in the door and

thought about all the grand times that were there," he said.

"But by the late 1960s it was just a place at the beach where you could rent a surf mat and get a good hot dog. It was finally torn down in 1973 and there is a condo there now."

They say of the Lumina that up those broad steps walked the prettiest girls in the world. Those pretty girls are grandmothers now, but when they remember it, their eyes still shine like the lights of the Lumina once shone on the nights of their youth.

Jefferson Davis' Black Friend

He was a trusted confidant of a president, a successful businessman, a political leader, a public servant and an eyewitness to the most momentous event in our national history. He served his nation with loyalty and dignity, but now he lies in a unmarked grave on the edge of Raleigh.

His name was James Jones and State Capitol historian Raymond Beck supplied the details of his life.

Jones was born in Raleigh in 1831 during a time of slavery, but he was never a slave. He was a free man all his life.

In 1862, when Federal forces were closing in on Richmond, the capitol of the Confederacy, President Jefferson Davis sent his wife, Varina, and his children to live on the grounds of St. Mary's College in Raleigh until the danger passed. It was during that summer that James Jones began a lifelong association with the first family of the Confederacy.

Hired as a coachman by Mrs. Davis, Jones was asked to return to Richmond with the family. He became the Confederate president's personal aide, driver and confidential courier. Davis entrusted his most secret messages to Jones, and Jones was there as Davis met with his Cabinet and military leaders.

And when the Confederacy fell in the spring of 1865, it was to Jones that Davis turned for help. He asked Jones to protect his family and take them south. Jones put the president's family in a carriage and drove them to Charlotte, where they remained for a few days, then went on to Georgia, where Davis and his family were reunited during their escape attempt.

Federal soldiers across the South were searching for the fleeing Confederate president, and they found him near the town of Irwinsville, Ga., early on the morning of May 11, 1865. It was Jones who first heard the approaching federal cavalry, and it was Jones who awoke his friend and president and told him the end had come. He was standing at Davis' side when he was captured.

Jones accompanied President Davis to Fortress Monroe in Virginia, and when Davis was locked in prison, Jones returned to Raleigh.

It was in Raleigh that he took an active part in the life of the city. He became a respected leader in the black community, serving as a delegate to two Freedman's Conventions. He organized the city's first black fire department. He was twice nominated by the Republican Party for a seat in the state's General Assembly, but declined the nomination both times.

He served on the Raleigh Board of Aldermen for 18 years and later organized the first black military unit in North Carolina. He also served several years as a Wake County deputy sheriff.

He was a successful businessman. His contracting firm built water systems, streets and streetcar lines across the South.

His loyalty and affection for Jefferson Davis and his family never wavered. He regularly corresponded with the family, and they with him, and he visited Davis on several occasions after the war.

He would have one last chance to honor the president to whom he had been so close. In 1893, President Davis' body was moved from Alabama to Hollywood Cemetery in Richmond. It would be the last chance the ordinary people of the South would have to pay homage to the man who had led the Confederacy through those four frightful years of war. His body lay in state in each of the Southern state capitols as it moved slowly north to Virginia.

Jones heard about the slow procession of Davis' body, and he hurried to his hometown of Raleigh to be here when the body arrived. He asked, and was given permission, to drive the funeral hearse that carried Davis' body to and from the state Capitol on May 30, 1883.

He also was on hand when the cornerstone of Davis' monument was laid in Richmond. He met Mrs. Davis there, and shortly thereafter, she sent him Davis' prized walking stick. Jones later donated the walking stick and a candleholder from the Davis home to the North Carolina Museum of History.

Jones spent his later years in Washington as a staff member of the U.S. Senate. He died in 1921 at the age of 90 and was buried in Mount Hope Cemetery on the outskirts of Raleigh. The cemetery has been heavily vandalized, and no tombstone now marks the grave of this remarkable man.

Disappearance of a Town

Catch Me Eye

Don't bother to look for this quaintly named community on any map. It disappeared from the face of Eastern North Carolina in a blinding flash at exactly 2:57 a.m. March 7, 1942.

There have been many spectacular accidents at what is now the intersection of U.S. 301 and U.S. 70-A between Smithfield and Selma in Johnston County, but nothing to compare with what happened that early Saturday morning.

It began as a serious, but routine, traffic accident. A car driven by Mrs. Minnie Lewis of Raleigh was involved in a collision with a truck at the intersection. A fire broke out after the accident, and Mrs. Lewis died of injuries received in the accident and the fire.

But the real horror was yet to come.

It was an intense fire, and firemen from surrounding areas fought it as best they could with the limited equipment they had. They knew disaster was possible because the truck was loaded with 30,000 pounds of high explosives.

Finally, there was nothing left for the firemen to do but pull away and wait for the fire to burn itself out. Crowds gathered to watch the blaze. Gurkin's Tavern was nearby, and the regulars were outside watching the growing blaze. The Talton Hotel was at the intersection, and two of Mrs. Lewis' children had been taken into the hotel to be treated for their wreck injuries. Some of the spectators were standing at Luke Capps' gas station, watching the excitement.

Highway patrolmen had tried without success to control the crowd, but there was little they could do.

At 2:57 a.m., two hours after the wreck, came the explosion officials had feared — and a community died.

It was a gigantic explosion. The Talton Hotel collapsed and was set ablaze. Gurkin's Tavern was demolished. Capps' gas station erupted in flames. George Stroupe of Gastonia and Cecil Propst of Lawndale were driving by the burning truck when it exploded, and they were killed instantly.

Mrs. R.L. Holloman, a 62-year-old woman who operated the Talton Hotel, was in the lobby helping take care of the original wreck victims. She was so injured in the explosion that wrecked the hotel and set it afire that she died a few days later.

Willie Howell, a Goldsboro taxi driver, was staying at the Talton Hotel as were sisters Jessie and Thelma Holloway. Thelma was injured by falling bricks and timbers, but she managed to escape death by leaping through a wall of fire. The bodies of Willie Howell and Jessie Holloway were found in the debris.

Buck Mitchell, a local man, was one of the spectators who were watching the fire when the explosion came. He was killed instantly.

Seven people were dead and 56 were injured. All of the businesses at the intersection were gone. Every window in Selma, about a mile away, was broken. The Selma Cotton Mill had 900 windows broken, and $10,000 worth of stained glass windows at the Selma Methodist Church were shattered. Parts of the ammunition truck were blown a mile and a half away by the explosion, which raised a fireball that could be seen and heard 50 miles away in Fayetteville. A total of 17 cars were destroyed in the blast and subsequent fire.

There were heroes aplenty that gruesome night. Two Marines were riding with the Lewis family when the original wreck happened. Marine Bernard Rosenberg was in the back seat when the wreck took place, and he climbed over the seat and escaped. But he realized others were still in the burning car, and he fought his way back inside. He made two trips to grab the two small Lewis children, Bobbie and Charlie, from the back seat and throw them into a nearby ditch. He went back a third time and pulled Mrs. Lewis out. A fourth time he went back, this time to get Odie Lewis, Mrs. Lewis' husband. He thought everyone was out then until he missed his buddy, fellow Marine Jimmy Blackstrom. He raced back into the flames a fifth time to save his friend.

Smithfield fireman Bill Norton, who had joined the department only a few days before, was another hero. He went into the burning hotel to rescue the two Lewis children for a second time. They had been taken into the hotel for safety and were trapped again when the explosion demolished the building. He and fire chief E.L. Woodall also brought Mrs. Holloman, the hotel manager, to safety, but she died of her injuries a few days later.

A total of 17 houses were so damaged that the families who lived in them were left homeless. The crater caused by the blast

was 50 feet across and 20 feet deep.
Catch Me Eye was gone.

The State's Stormy Past

Marshallberg

My pal Sonny Williamson truly is blessed. He gets to live in the real Down East, that wild and beautiful peninsula of Carteret County between Beaufort and Cedar Island. He gets to eat clam chowder and hush puppies made by his wife, Jenny, and he gets to collect wonderful stories.

He has written several books about that most wonderful part of North Carolina, and he shares them with me from time to time. And I like nothing more than passing them on to you.

Recently, I saw in the paper where scientists were predicting a busy hurricane season. They seem to do that every year, and I suspect the reason is that hurricanes long have been a spectacular part of our coast's colorful history. We haven't had a really big one in many years, and newcomers might be lulled into thinking we're overdoing it with our dire warnings. But let me, a survivor of the infamous Hurricane Hazel of the early 1950s, tell you they are not to be taken lightly.

Hurricanes get names now, but the one the old people still tell tales about Down East was one known only as the 1899 August Storm. According to Sonny, here is what happened in that deadly time:

It was the first week of August. The mullets were beginning their run, and it was time for the isolated fishermen of Down East to fish or go hungry all winter.

The storm began Aug. 2 off the west coast of Africa. By Aug. 5, it was a hurricane, moving across the Atlantic. By Aug. 8, it was hitting Puerto Rico, and five days later, it passed near Miami. On the morning of Aug. 17, with winds approaching 130 miles per hour, it slammed into Cape Lookout.

The fishermen did not know it was coming. It was the season for storms, but the bad weather they saw on the horizon looked like just another "mullet blow," the freshening winds and seas that often accompanied fishing time. It would make the mullets move and send the shallow-draft sailing sharpies dancing across the waters of the sounds.

Seven boats set sail from Wit (now Sealevel) and Piney Point (now Stacy) on the morning of Aug. 15. They were heading for Swan Island, where the Neuse River meets Pamlico Sound. They would camp there and fish the local waters.

They sailed off that morning in a line with John Styron at the helm of the lead boat. They waved goodbye to their families at the dock and went off into legend. There were the four Smith brothers from Piney Point: Elijah, 40; Wallace, 38; Kilby, 33; and John, 31. From Wit came John Styron, 46; Joe Lewis, 25, and his brother John, about 24; Joe Salter, 43, and his two younger brothers, John and Bart. There were Henry and Jim Willis, Macajah Rose, 32, and William Henry Salter, 15.

Two other fishing crews saw the seven boats set sail that day. Their crews had decided to wait, and that decision would save their lives.

The storm clouds were behind them as they set sail for Swan Island, but they were experienced sailors, who were sure they could make it. They had no way of knowing the size of the storm they could see coming.

The storm hit full force on the night of Aug. 17. The fishermen had ridden out the storm on Swan Island, and when morning came Aug. 18, they were cold, wet and hungry. But because the motto of all professional fishermen is "a wet butt and a hungry gut," they were not overly concerned.

Then the weather cleared. It was calm and sunny all at once, although bad weather seemed to encircle them completely. They decided to use the good weather and make for home. No one knew that they were not safe, that they were simply in the eye of a deadly hurricane.

They only had to go 10 miles.

The little flotilla made it three miles before the storm hit again, worse than ever. One of the crew members who stayed on Swan Island recalled: "We knew the storm was a-coming back and pretty soon she shifted to the nor'west and when we looked around, we could see the Neuse River over the marsh on Raccoon Island. Looked like a wall o'water, 10 or 12 feet high a-coming right down on us. We thought we were goners."

The men who had set sail for home all died that day in the storm. It took months, but they eventually found all the bodies but that of John Lewis. Among them, they left 10 widows and 20 children.

It was a disaster of unprecedented scope in the small coastal villages where everyone knew or was related to the brave men in the small boats, and even now, when men can track and predict hurricanes with precision, the old people Down East pay close attention.

They still remember the big one.

Tiny 'Doll Girl' of Aviation

Henderson

I've always wished I had gotten to know "Tiny" Broadwick. I've known about her daring exploits for years, but time and distance always kept me from having a chance to know her.

She was quite a woman. Now her derring-do is recorded only in musty newspaper clippings and fading photographs, but the thrills she must have known still make me look at the old pictures with awe.

Her name then was Georgia Thompson. She was 15 years old in 1908 and worked 12 hours a day in a Henderson textile mill. Times had been tough for the girl who was but 5 feet tall.

She was separated from her husband and was trying to raise a child while little more than a child herself. One day she went to a carnival between Durham and Raleigh, and there she met Charlie Broadwick and his hot-air balloon.

Broadwick had quite an act. He would build a fire beneath his giant balloon, and when it was full of hot air, it would rise slowly into the sky. It was a marvel for local folks. Remember, that it was only five years before that the Wright brothers had flown their flimsy little airplane at Kitty Hawk.

And then, to the amazement of the crowd, a man would jump out of the balloon with a homemade parachute. No one had seen such a thing, and Georgia Thompson decided that was for her.

"I was always something of a tomboy," she told an interviewer years later. "And that balloon act simply fascinated me."

She was so fascinated that she talked Broadwick into hiring her, a 15-year-old girl with no experience. He did, and the legendary "Doll Girl" of aviation was on her way.

She took Broadwick's last name as her stage name. She was so little that "Tiny" seemed inevitable, and she thrilled crowds across the country as Tiny Broadwick and became a national star.

It was harrowing work. The balloons were homemade, and if the fire got too hot they would split. The parachutes were homemade as well, and more than one of them ripped. But the plucky little girl never got seriously hurt.

It was in 1913, after traveling America with the balloon act, that Tiny Broadwick of Henderson leaped into the record books.

That summer, just 10 years after the first man flew, Tiny became the first woman to jump out of an airplane. Some reports even say she was the first person, man or woman, to jump from an airplane.

They were 2,000 feet over Los Angeles on June 21, 1913. Airplane manufacturer Glenn Martin was at the controls. Tiny was hanging from a seat rigged behind the engine and beneath the cockpit when she tripped a lever and drifted to the ground. Later that summer she jumped over Chicago and landed in the frigid waters of Lake Michigan, the first person ever to make a water landing. People were amazed, and thousands flocked to see her as she and Martin toured the country.

The Army had a few airplanes then, and Martin was trying to sell the military on the idea of putting parachutes on its pilots. He called them "a life preserver for the air" and tried to convince the Army to buy them to save the lives of pilots who flew the rickety aircraft of the day.

Tiny traveled the country for 14 years doing her show. She jumped day and night, often carrying torches and flares to light her descent in the darkened sky. In all, she jumped more than 1,000 times and never received more than a few scratches and one broken wrist.

But times were changing. A World War had come and gone, and airplanes were becoming more commonplace. No one wanted to see a little girl no bigger than a minute jump out of airplanes.

Tiny settled in California where she became a folk hero to sky divers and fliers. They, better than anyone else, knew how important she was as a brave role model in the early days of flying and barnstorming.

She came to Raleigh to visit in 1974, and when a reporter asked her if she'd ever had a reserve parachute in case the one she was wearing failed, she gave him an answer that says a lot about just how brave she was.

Yes, she said, there was a reserve parachute. They kept one back in the hangar in case the one she was wearing got wet or muddy during the show.

So Tiny Broadwick became the guinea pig. She jumped over Los Angeles again as generals watched.

"However, they didn't take to the idea too quickly," she remembered later. "It seems they were afraid that if the pilots were equipped with life preservers, they would jump out at the first indication of trouble and let the plane crash. And at that time the United States only had about three airplanes."

Cross of a Native Son

Ocracoke

It is a simple, handmade cross, but it occupies a special place on both the altar of the Ocracoke United Methodist Church and in the legends of the people of this island village.

How it came to be here is one of those Ocracoke Island stories that leave you wondering how in the world it could have happened. And as with all good legends, there are a couple of different versions and some of the details may differ in the telling, but the hard facts themselves are pretty amazing.

It is the story of James Baughm Gaskill, a seagoing man from Ocracoke. Gaskill was a native, the son of Bill and Anne Gaskill. Bill and Anne ran the old Pamlico Inn, one of the first places available for outsiders to stay when they came to visit the island in the days before roads and ferries.

Young Jim was born in 1919 and, like most boys of Ocracoke, was a familiar sight around the town, on the beaches and on the waters surrounding the island. As with so many of those who came before him, it was the sea that finally drew him away from Ocracoke. Jim's father died in 1936 and his mother died in 1940, so it was not surprising to anyone that he left the island and went to sea. But he would return in a most mysterious way.

Jim joined the Merchant Marine and by 1942 had risen to the rank of second mate. By March of that year, he was working on the Caribsea, a steamer hauling manganese in her hold and balsa wood lashed to her deck.

It was the night of March 11, 1942. The Caribsea was heading north up the coast, pushed along by a gale blowing astern. It was a dangerous place to be that night.

The United States had been at war for three months, and since January, German submarines had been marauding along the coast at will, sinking dozens of unarmed merchant ships.

It was nearing midnight, and Second Mate Gaskill was coming to the end of his 8 p.m. to midnight watch. It was not the first time he had sailed these waters, and his routine was to always be on the bridge when the ship passed the historic Ocracoke Lighthouse off to port. It was a flicker of home for him, and he liked to see it pass.

But not this night. Exhausted from fighting to keep the ship steady in the storm and weary from constantly watching for submarines, Gaskill turned in when his relief arrived on the bridge at eight minutes until midnight. He went to his quarters and went to bed.

The torpedo struck the Caribsea moments after he fell into this bunk. There were 26 men on board and only eight of them were saved. Second Mate Jim Baughm Gaskill was not among them.

The people of Ocracoke were used to wreckage washing ashore in those war days. Most of it was trash, but enough of it was salvageable to make it worth walking the beach to see what came ashore.

But most of the wreckage came ashore on the ocean side of the island. Most but not all.

No one can say for certain now who found the board, about 18 inches wide and five feet long, but it came riding the tide in from the sea, through Ocracoke Inlet, turned right into the waters of Pamlico Sound and came to rest beside the deck at the Pamlico Inn, where Jim Baughm Gaskill had been raised. Whoever found it — some say it was Jim's cousin — turned it over and found the gilded nameplate from the Caribsea, the ship that had taken Jim Gaskill to his death.

It had traveled miles through an open, storm-tossed sea to land where he had lived, bringing the unmistakable message that he was dead.

But there was more.

On the door of the bridge of the Caribsea hung eight picture frames holding the licenses of the officers of the ship. Only one of those eight picture frames made it intact to the oceanside beach at Ocracoke. It was the mariner's license of James Baughm Gaskill.

He still had family living on the island, and they decided that the strange events of his death and wreckage coming ashore should be memorialized. They took the picture frame to neighbor Homer Howard who used part of it, as well as other wreckage from the Caribsea, to build a simple, rustic cross atop a pedestal. On the plaque on the front of the pedestal are engraved the words: "In memory of Capt. James B. Gaskill, July 2, 1919 — March 11, 1942. This cross constructed from salvage from the ship upon which Capt. Gaskill lost his life."

The nameplate of the Caribsea that washed ashore in front of his childhood home now hangs on the wall of the Cape Hatteras National Seashore Visitors Center in Ocracoke.

His body was never found, although a tombstone bearing his name stands near the Ocracoke Lighthouse.

It's Bad News When . . .

Hurricane Bob was snorting and puffing and blowing rain outside the bar as the regulars stepped around the half-dozen buckets and cups scattered to catch the leaks. They tried not to glance at the ceiling that is held up by nothing more substantial than fervent hopes.

Down at the corner of the bar — near the very spot where the best hot dogs in Raleigh used to be served until some overeager columnist, who should have kept his pencil in his pocket, wrote about them and brought the swift arm of the germ sheriffs down on that unlicensed little wiener stand — a man with long hair and a long white beard waved his arms and quoted the "Rubaiyat" of Omar Khayyam when he wasn't reading from a Peanuts comics collection.

Up by the pool table, a dollar bill changed hands at game's end. The players were not gambling on the outcome of the game, of course. Gambling was not allowed at the 42nd Street Tavern, the finest beer joint in the English-speaking world. They must have been giving change. Yeah, that's it.

It was late on a hot, stormy afternoon. Fatalism hung heavy in the humid air.

I hate it when a bartender calls me at home and tells me he's been crying all day. What do I say to him? I'm supposed to be telling him my hard-luck stories after I've had a snootful, not listening to him moan and groan. But B-Square is not your ordinary bartender.

His real name is Bob Black. The B-Square business is complicated, but it has to do with his initials. You'd have to know higher math to figure it out, and it's simply not worth the trouble.

Just accept it and understand that nobody in the world knows more about what it takes to run a good beer joint than Bob Black. He has spent enough time on the paying side of the bar to know how it ought to be done, and he has used that insider's knowledge to run a joint where a man or woman can go drink and enjoy it. He has not made a lot of money, but he has got a lot of friends, and he gets to drink at wholesale prices and that counts for a lot, or ought to.

The 42nd Street was not a nightclub with flashing lights or some fern bar where singles gather to meet, or some college drinkery where the smell of zit cream overpowers honest beer and sweat. It was certainly not a lounge or a pub. This was an honest beer joint where men and women of high caliber came to drink and pass the time with congenial souls. Getting quietly drunk with friends was the premier form of entertainment there.

"Cheers" is a fictional bar in Boston. The 42nd Street, which Bob thinks is the oldest continuously operated beer joint in North Carolina, was the real thing. It was not like the TV Cheers. It was better. It was as real as the drip down the back of your neck when a new leak breaks out.

It was also going to close in 30 days.

No one knew exactly how long it had been since J.C. Watson hooked three old houses together at the corner of Jones and West streets in Raleigh and opened an oyster bar. Charlie Craven, a man who knew honest bars, wrote in 1974 when they got rid of the oysters that it had been open 45 years then. It has been legally selling cold beer since Dec. 5, 1933, the day Prohibition ended.

The place looked like it, too. Never one for tony decor, it was a mean and intimidating place on the outside, a place that strangers passed by on dark nights. But the customers smiled even when they were sober.

Inside, it was not much better-looking. It was black everywhere it could be painted and dark wood otherwise.

But to borrow from Bogey, of all the joints in the all the towns in all the world, I'm happy I walked into there. I made a promise when they accepted me into the fold never to write about the

42nd Street Tavern, because they didn't want the place discovered and ruined. With a couple of lapses — the hot dogs and the juke box were just too good to ignore — I kept the faith and my seat at the bar.

Bob Black loved his run-down little place and the people who made it their home and his. He was looking for another place so we could all pick up and move on Sept. 1, the day after the lease ended and the bulldozers rolled and we had us one last party.

The place was old and rundown, and people of high breeding turned their noses up at it. And yeah, if I owned the building I'd probably have torn it down, too.

But I sure do miss it.

A New Year's Eve Reprieve

It was New Year's Eve 1968 in Vietnam, and Nick Rowe was being taken to die.

James N. "Nick" Rowe, now a Southern Pines resident and a lieutenant colonel at Fort Bragg, had been a prisoner of the Viet Cong for more than five years in late 1968. Captured while on a military operation with South Vietnamese forces, the Green Beret had successfully lied to his captors and saved his life.

"I told them I was an engineer," he said. "I told them I built roads and bridges but I didn't know which end of a rifle to use. I had expected my cover story to last six months, but it had lasted for five years.

"Then a peace group in the United States put together a biography of me that identified me as Special Forces, and the information had reached the Viet Cong.

"They brought me into a building and sat me on the floor. The senior officer said I had been lying to them for five years and that I would be executed. But first I'd be moved to another camp."

There were six Viet Cong with Rowe as they moved out that last day. Suddenly there were American helicopters overhead.

They began to run for cover. Rowe was wearing the same black pajama-like clothes as his captors, and there was no way the Americans could know that among the men they were chasing across the marshy countryside was one of their own.

Rowe was at the rear of the group, followed only by a guard he had nicknamed Porky.

"We had nicknamed all the guards," he said. "That made them seem less threatening to us. Porky was the most innocuous of all of them. He was never meant to be a soldier. He was not intentionally cruel. If he was ordered to beat us he would, but his punches never hurt as much as the others' did. He didn't have his heart in it."

Rowe and Porky became separated from the other guards. Suddenly, there were just the two of them.

"Porky was in front, and I was carrying his radio," Rowe said. "I knew this was it. If they held me I was going to be killed. This was my last chance.

"Porky was trying to crawl through some reeds, and I reached up and pushed the magazine release on his weapon. The magazine fell into the water but he didn't know it. He pulled his weapon around and saw that the magazine was gone. He looked at me with a sick grin, the way the Coyote looks at the Roadrunner just before the disaster hits in the cartoons. And he said, in Vietnamese, 'You wouldn't happen to know where my magazine is, would you?' "

Moments later, Rowe hit Porky and made his dash to freedom.

"I was trying for his carotid artery," Rowe said. "That would have cut off the blood to his brain and he would have been unconscious for several minutes. I wanted to take him out with me. I wanted him to see what our life was like.

"I caught him as he fell and laid his head on some reeds so he wouldn't fall into the water. But as I did I saw I had crushed his trachea.

"I looked down at him and said, 'I'm sorry, Porky, I didn't mean to do that.' "

Rowe ran for open ground so the helicopters would see him.

"I reached an open area and was waving my mosquito net over my head. The first chopper came over and fired at me but missed. The second one was coming in on another pass."

On board one helicopter was Maj. Dave Thompson. He saw the man in the open below and ordered, "Wait, I want a VC prisoner."

Then door gunner Mike Thompson looked at the man dressed in the enemy uniform and noticed he had a beard. He shouted, "Wait a minute, sir, that's an American."

The chopper settled to the ground and Rowe dashed for it,

leaping onto the cold metal floor and shouting, "Go! Go! Go!"

"The chopper cleared the trees and I saw the horizon for the first time after five years in the jungle," Rowe said. "I had forgotten how big the world was.

"In just a minute the co-pilot asked me if I was Nick Rowe. I said yes, and he handed me his earphones. . . . He said, 'Welcome home, Nick, welcome home, buddy.' "

Hospitality for Boaters

Elizabeth City

Ruby Kramer loved the 52 rose bushes in her yard, and she would have loved what her husband, Joe, is doing with them now.

Each afternoon, as the yachts plying the Dismal Swamp Canal and the Intracoastal Waterway begin tying up at the public dock in Elizabeth City, Joe Kramer is there presenting homegrown roses to every woman on every boat.

"I hated to see the roses go to waste," Joe said. "My wife died three years ago, and the roses were her hobby. I really don't know why, but I started taking them to the ladies on the boats about a year and a half ago."

That courtly act of Southern hospitality, just a rose in a bud vase for a tired seagoing lady, has grown to where this Pasquotank River port is famous all over the East Coast as the most cordial of harbors.

The credit goes to Kramer, a 76-year-old retired county school budget officer and his lifelong friend, 71-year-old Fred Fearing, a veteran of 38 years as a walking mailman. Buddies for almost 70 years, they have appointed themselves as town greeters.

"We started coming down here at night just to walk around and look at the boats and meet the people," Joe said. "It grew from that."

And how it has grown. Imagine yourself sailing up to the docks after a long day on the water. There you'll meet the ebullient Fred Fearing and the quieter Joe Kramer. Fred will hand you a packet of information, including a walking tour of the town and a free daily newspaper. Joe will take a fast head count and be ready with his roses for the ladies.

They'll welcome you to town, tell you a joke or two, point out the nearby car lot where Mayor Ty Newell works and where you can get a free courtesy car to run errands or sightsee. Or they'll take you anywhere you need to go.

Then they'll invite you to the daily wine and cheese party they give near the docks.

"We always invite about the same number of local people to the party as we have boaters," Fred said. "That way, the boaters get to meet us, and we meet them. Many times, the local people invite the boaters home with them or to church, and they go. We've got a waiting list of people who want to come to the party."

"This is unbelievable," said a grinning Robert Scott of Terre Haute, Ind. He had arrived on board the 48-foot yacht Sea Pen with friends Mildred and O.W. Pendergast. "I had forgotten there could be places like this. We just went over and got a car, and they didn't even ask us our names. They just gave us the keys."

Oct. 14, 1984, was a lucky day for the boaters seeking shelter from the rough seas of Hurricane Josephine. It was on that Sunday, standing in the churchyard after services, that Fred turned to Joe and said, "Let's have a Thanksgiving party for the boaters."

One had some chips, and the other had some wine. They hauled it down to the docks, and the first party was on.

None of this has cost the city a dime. Shirley Mays organized a drive to install the 14 boat slips at a city park on Water Street. She got local businesses and people to donate $1,500 each to install the slips. Joe and Fred have taken on welcoming duties as their own. The mayor donates the cars, and the local paper gives the newspapers. And the hundreds of boats spend an average of $150 while in the free slips.

Fred said he and Joe refuse to take donations to pay for the food or the vases for the roses.

"If we don't take anyone's money we can do it like we want to," Fred said. "We're not obligated to anyone. We won't take money from them, but I tell them if we find it on Joe's car seat we won't know where it came from. We find money in his car all the time. One time we found $40."

"I even find vases on my porch," Joe said. "The other ones I buy at yard sales." Sure, it's no big deal, just a couple of old guys whose wives died three years ago who refuse to sit home and watch television all day. Just a couple of guys looking for a way to keep busy.

But when the Sea Pen pulled in, and Mildred Pendergast leaned over the rail to take that bright red rose from Joe's outstretched hand, you should have seen her smile.

Outer Banks Christmas Spirit

Rodanthe

There were pretty ladies to be danced with, steaming oysters to be eaten and liquor to be drunk, but first there was Ed Corley to think about.

Ed Corley is a fisherman, like so many of those who had gathered in this tiny Outer Banks village for the annual party they call Old Christmas. He was working on a trawler off the coast of Oregon state when the nightmare that is so much a part of life out here came true.

"They found one of the crewmen from his trawler half in his survival suit, but he was dead," Joey O'Neal said. "They found the captain in his suit, and he was fine. But they haven't found Ed yet. They went down on New Year's Eve."

So Joey, also a fisherman, got up on the stage as the band was setting up to play and asked the islanders to bow their heads for a minute and think about Ed and maybe, if they felt like it, to say a quiet prayer for one of their own, alive or dead, floating in a cold ocean somewhere.

"My brother was a fisherman, and he drowned two years ago," Joey said."So I guess it means more to me when I hear about a neighbor lost at sea."

Neither Joey O'Neal's somber beginning for this year's old Christmas celebration, nor the rain that came later, seemed to dampen the party spirit that marks the event. These folks live with rough seas and death year-round and the Saturday closest to the 12th Day of Christmas has been party time for much longer than anyone can remember.

You hear talk that it has been going on for 200 years. Maybe. But no one really knows.

"All I can tell you is that my grandmother died in 1955 when she was 86 years old and she told me that it had been going on for all of her life and before," said Don Edwards, one of the organizers for this year's event. "What's that, at least 116 years? You can take it from there.''

In any case, whether it is 116 years old or 250 years old, it is the longest-running annual party most anyone has ever heard of.

There was a time, way back there, when it had perhaps a vestige of religious meaning. The legend goes — and legend is as good as facts out here — that back in 1752, when the king of England changed the calendars and moved Christmas from Jan. 6 to Dec. 25, the folks living on the islands didn't get the word so they continued to celebrate Christmas on Jan. 6. And once they did hear about the change, they didn't care for it and, being the stubborn types they are, decided to continue their old ways, or at least a semblance of them.

Outside the Rodanthe Community Center, which in bygone days saw duty as the village's one-room schoolhouse, Larry Midgett supervised the roasting of 38 bushels of incredibly succulent oysters.

He and his crew shoveled bushel after bushel of oysters onto the grill of an Eastern North Carolina-style pig cooker, which looks like a large oil drum split in half the long way and hinged on one side. They wet them down, placed wet burlap bags over them, lowered the lid and let the oysters steam in their own juices until they popped open. That done, they shoveled the hot shells onto rude wooden tables where serious oyster eaters, armed with their own oyster knives, devoured them.

Take it from a veteran old oyster eater: Standing around an Outer Banks roast, opening your own oysters, with juice running down your forearms and chin, the lilting accent of Banker speech ringing in your ears and eating oysters that just hours before were resting peacefully on the ocean bottom is not a bad way to say goodbye to the holiday season.

Meet L.A. 'Speed' Riggs

Rocky Mount

There was only one auctioneer's job open at the warehouse that day in 1935, and five people wanted it.

The oldest men went first and showed what they could do by auctioning off two rows of tobacco each. Then it was time for the brash 18-year-old kid to do his stuff.

''I started off down the first row, and in five minutes the people watching were dancing a jig," he said. "People were laughing and clapping their hands and yelling, 'Hire the kid, hire the kid.' "

They hired the kid that day and made him the youngest tobacco auctioneer in the country. Now, more that 50 years later L.A. "Speed" Riggs is still the most famous tobacco auctioneer there ever was.

"I went to a tobacco warehouse in Maysville with my father when I was 7 years old," Riggs said. "I heard an auctioneer for the first time and I was captivated my it. I knew then that was what I wanted to be. But I didn't want to be just an auctioneer. I wanted to be the best auctioneer."

His was a career that in two years took him from a dusty North Carolina tobacco warehouse to the bright lights of New York City, where he became the spokesman for Lucky Strike cigarettes from 1937 to 1970.

Speed Riggs' name may not ring a bell at first. But the sing-song auctioneer's chant he used — the one that ended with the ringing "Sold, American!" — was as famous in its day as "Where's the beef?"

Speed Riggs changed forever the way tobacco auctioneers sound. Now they all sound like he did.

"I used to go to the warehouses and listen to the auctioneers," he said over a plate of barbecue. "They talked the sale in a kind of guttural language. I'd go home and practice and one day, walking down a road, I tried something different. I tried singing the words and I knew I had it. I could do 590 words a minute by the time I was 17."

He knew he was good, but he didn't know how good. Within two years after that first job in Goldsboro, Speed had made it to the big market in Durham. He had gotten a lot of attention and publicity with his lilting, singing chant. One day, George Washington Hill, then president of American Tobacco Co. in New York, hopped a train and came south to hear the sensational auctioneer who was making all the waves.

"I saw a group of men wearing homburg hats watching me work in the Liberty Warehouse," he said. "So I got faster and faster. Then Mr. Hill walked over and said, 'I want you to come to New York and be the voice of Lucky Strikes on the radio.' I got on the train that night."

That was a Friday. The next night Speed Riggs stepped in front of a microphone during a commercial break on Lucky Strike's "Your Hit Parade" and let it rip. He never made his living selling tobacco again. At the age of 20, in the midst of the Depression, the fifth-grade dropout from North Carolina was making $450 a week and was a national celebrity.

"They gave me a 20-year exclusive contract with an option to renew for another 20 years," he said. "I had it made."

Year after year, Speed Riggs' fame spread. His name became synonymous with Lucky Strikes, the best-selling cigarette of all. In 1941 they did a survey, and 84 percent of the American public identified him with Lucky Strike.

He traveled the country for Lucky Strike, giving parties, interviews, and speeches, and doing charity auctions. During World War II, he sold $218 million in War Bonds in eight months, including $7 million in one day on Boston Common. His "Lucky Strike means fine tobacco" was part of the language. It was so familiar that it was shortened to "LS / MFT" and everyone still knew what it meant.

He made it into the movies in Hollywood in the mid-1950s, appearing in 11 films with friends like Dale Robertson and Glenn Ford. Once he even got to play the heavy and rip the bodice of '50s sexpot Yvonne DeCarlo in a forgettable Clark Gable slavery epic.

The fame lasted until 1970 when cigarette commercials were ordered off radio and television. His time in the spotlight had come to an end. He began a successful non-profit organization called "Your Community Fund" in Fullerton, Calif., that taught job skills to handicapped and underprivileged clients.

"It makes you feel good to walk into a warehouse and listen to the auctioneers imitating you," he said. "It makes you feel good to know you created something that has lasted. There never was a night when I haven't thanked God for the advantages he gave me."

And yes, he still smokes Lucky Strikes.

The Old Man in the Woods

The old man hadn't been around for a while, but no one thought much about it. They knew he was a walking man who had fallen in love with long distance many years ago.

When he was around, they'd often see him sitting in the sun near the grove of trees where he kept a spotless little camp. He had a tent he had picked up somewhere in his travels, and he had built himself a neat little fireplace and stove from rocks he picked up down by the creek.

No one bothered him when he was in the place they thought of as his home. The man who owned the grove of trees where the old man camped had long ago given his permission for him to live there when he was in those parts.

He was a friendly old man. Boys from the neighborhood liked to ride their bikes out from town and spend time talking to him. He would tell them stories about places he had been and show them how to cook the rabbits they would catch in their rabbit boxes. He would tell them about the birds in the woods, and sometimes he'd tell them a story that came from one of the books he kept around. His favorite book was full of stories of the Arabian Nights.

And then one day, without warning, he would be gone. He'd fold up his tent and strap it on the back of the old pack he carried, and they would see him walking down the road with that long stride of his. Sometimes folks would offer him a ride, and he would take it and he would ride as far as they would take him, but all he would say when they asked him where he was going was, "I'm going to walk around some."

It was usually months before he would be back. Then one day he would show up, and they would see a thin curl of smoke coming from his camp fire and he would be home.

He worked some, but you had to ask him if he would do it. He would come and clean out your gutters or help you bale hay or do some painting, but he never asked for work or for a handout. No one knew how he got his money, but sometimes they would see him at the post office, and folks figured he got some money that way, but they didn't know where it came from.

It was about this time of the year, and no one had seen him for a while. Then one day some boys setting rabbit boxes saw the tell-tale smoke and went up to see the old man.

He was sitting there as usual, leaning back on a stump in the warm December sun, and he wasn't alone.

She looked to be about 18 or so, but the baby she was holding in her arms made the boys think she must be older than that.

There were two tents in the clearing this time, and some cloth diapers were hanging across a rope that ran between the two small tents.

He introduced the boys to the girl and her baby, but he didn't tell them much about them. He was as friendly as ever and just as private.

One of the boys told his parents about the old man being back and how he had brought a girl and a baby back with him. Folks got to talking about it in church, and some folks said somebody ought to do something about that. An old man living in the woods is one thing, but this business with the baby was another matter.

The welfare lady went out to investigate, and that's when the whole story came out. She was 18, and she had had the baby without a husband around. Her folks didn't like that and they had made her leave home. She had been on the road alone when she had met the old man, and he had taken care of her and her child and brought them to his clearing to share his life.

There were some who said they ought to put the baby in an orphanage and run that tramp of a girl out of town. It was for the good of the baby, they said. Others weren't so sure that was the right thing to do, but they didn't speak up.

The welfare lady went to a judge and told him how this poor little baby was living in a tent in the woods and asked for permission to take it away and find it a good home.

No one asked the old man how he felt, and they didn't ask the girl, either. The judge didn't bother to go out and see the camp and how neat and clean it was and how they had plenty of blankets and sleeping bags and food for all of them.

The judge said the welfare could take the baby. It was for its own good, he said.

So the sheriff took the welfare lady out to the camp, but it was empty when they got there. Somebody had told the old man and the girl what was going on in town, and they had left for parts unknown.

The old man never came back. No one ever knew what had happened to him or to the girl he had befriended or, most of all, to the baby.

But one of those boys who used to listen to the old man's stories and who met the girl and the baby has often wondered.

"I hope they made it OK," Raleigh's Mike Schlosser said when he told me the story of what happened near his hometown of Cumberland, Md., 20 years ago.

"He was a good man, and he would have taken good care of that girl and her baby. After they left, my parents and some other people in town said they would have been glad to help them find a house.

"My father was a mailman and he said the old man used to get a check every month. He could have lived in a house, but he'd rather live in the woods. After they left, the checks stopped coming."

Fond Memories Blossom

Rocky Mount

Janis Cooper was the teacher all of the third graders at Englewood Elementary School talked about on the first day of school each year.

"They really didn't want to be in her room," Englewood principal Joan Hawley said with a smile. "She had a reputation of being a hard teacher, and she was. But after two or three days they loved her."

Miss Cooper was tough as leather. She put up with no nonsense in her classes. Rules were rules, and they would be followed to the letter. You raise your hand before you talk. You keep all four legs of your chair on the floor at all times. You bring your own pencil to class. You sit up straight. The rules were posted on the wall and even though you were but 9 years old, you toed the line. Most of all, you learned.

"I think she even intimidated other teachers here," Mrs. Hawley said. "She was a stern woman. She wanted perfection for herself and expected it from other people."

Then Janis Cooper died in a wreck a month ago and the side of her that no one who didn't know her very well came out. Sure, they still tell stories about how tough she was in the classroom, but they temper them with the stories of her love.

"She had a special rapport with children whom no one else seemed to be able to reach," Mrs. Hawley said. "We had one boy who everyone thought was a bad boy, a troublemaker. But they got along very well. He kept saying, 'I wish she hadn't died, I wish she hadn't died.' "

The stories they remember most are about Miss Cooper and the school flag.

Every morning her class lined up and sang George M. Cohan's goose-bump raising, "Grand Old Flag". And every year she "volunteered" her class to be in charge of raising and lowering the school flag. Her class of third graders were drilled endlessly in how to honor the flag, how you never let so much as the hem touch the ground, how you raise it smartly and lower it with dignity and never, but never, let it get rained on.

"She kept an eagle eye on the weather," Mrs. Hawley said. "You let one drop of rain fall and there she'd go with her third-graders, trooping out to take down the flag. She'd make them fold it perfectly every time."

And Christmas pageants? Janis Cooper loved Christmas pageants. Every class is responsible for putting on an assembly program each year at Englewood and it was tradition that Miss Cooper's class would do the annual Christmas pageant.

"She wrote the play herself and made sure that every student in her class had a part," Mrs. Hawley said. "It wasn't just a walk-on part, either. Everybody had a speaking part."

A lot of people didn't know about the flowers, either. Janis and her mother, who also died in the wreck, ran a florist shop in Spring Hope and most folks figure they gave away as many flowers as they sold. One minister moved to town with his new bride and casually mentioned that they loved yellow roses. Every week from then on he found a bunch of yellow roses on his doorstep. The civic clubs in town often ordered flowers for their meetings, but no one but the treasurer ever realized they didn't get a bill.

"This school was Janis' life," Mrs. Hawley said. "She taught here for the 26 years this school has been open. She never traveled and she never married. She was 55 years old and she was in school every fall from the time she was 6 years old.

"Janis wasn't much of a hugger. She talked loud and had a sharp tongue, but when it came to teaching your children what they came to school to learn, it was Janis, hands down. Her students were always among the best-behaved and had the best handwriting of any class here. She touched a lot of lives here but she was not the warm, friendly kind who would receive the credit.

"She was so terrifically sincere. She knew what her job was and did everything she had to to get it done. Even those who didn't like her, admired her."

That's why the memorial for Janis Cooper is so perfect. She loved flowers, teaching and the flag and soon all of those will come together in front of Englewood. They are going to landscape the area around the flag pole with azaleas and a decorative bench and put in a plaque that reads "Janis Cooper, 1960-1986". Straight and to the point.

Miss Cooper, the hardest teacher in school, is the one they'll never forget at Englewood.

Wilton Welcomes the Torch

Wilton

It was not, everyone agreed, the biggest event ever to take place in this Granville County village.

That honor goes to the autumn night in 1979 when the Wilton clogging team returned home after winning the national Grange clogging championship in Lancaster, Pa.

But the three-minute visit of the U.S. Olympic Festival torch one Wednesday morning was, indisputably, the second biggest thing to ever happen in Wilton and one that will be talked about for a long time.

"We got together at church last Sunday and agreed that since the torch was coming through Wilton, we just had to do something about it," Lena Gooch said.

It was a fine thing they did, too.

They hung a big banner across the only intersection they have. They brought several gallons of pretty good lemonade that was served off the tailgate of a freshly washed pickup truck. And they borrowed some flags from an Oxford car dealer and waved them like crazy and generally shared a lot of small town love and good will. And the best thing was — no politicians made speeches.

You could tell good things were going to happen two hours before the torch arrived. By 9 a.m., retired school principal Bob Hunt already was pacing around in his cowboy boots, worrying about details and telling people what to do.

"Welcome to the City of Wilton," he said. "This is a fine city. Our biggest industry here is a two-stall car wash."

While calling it a city might be stretching things just a bit, Wilton does have two industries. There is the car wash and H.H. Kearney's Store. They also have one empty building. If there were ever 25 people in Wilton at one time, somebody would wonder what was going on.

"We used to have another store," Nan Hunt said. "Mr. Willie Gooch had this empty building and that was where the men used to leave their wives and go play setback. Several people tried to run it after he died, but they couldn't make a go of it."

Activity was at a fever pitch two hours before the torch arrived. Granville County commissioner Pete Averette had brought the flags and the plastic banner, which also was from

Oxford. And someone (no one would say who pulled the right strings) had convinced the telephone company to send a truck to hang the banner high in the air across the road.

But there was a problem with the flags. They were nice flags, but they were meant to stick on automobile radio antennae. So Nan Hunt used her kitchen curtain rods for flag sticks. They worked well.

The crowd was impressive. Some folks came from Creedmoor, some from Butner and one couple even came from Hillsborough. It was Wilton's once-in-a-lifetime tourist season.

"This is the only time I'll ever have a chance to see the torch," Cecil Keith of Creedmoor said. "I haven't seen it in 60 years and I'm not likely to see it again, so I came to Wilton." There were at least 200 people gathered by the intersection of N.C. 96 and N.C. 56 at 10 when the torch was due to arrive. The scene was akin to a church dinner, what with all the hugging, hand shaking and refrains of "How's your mama and them?"

The elderly and the shut-ins had been brought and front row spots were found for those in wheelchairs. Everyone fussed appropriately over them and made sure they had plenty of lemonade and a clear view. Lena Gooch and Bob Hunt kept the crowd almost awash in lemonade.

The torch was late, an hour and seven minutes late to be exact, but nobody cared. It was a fine, hot day so everyone drank the lemonade, visited and looked up the hill.

At 11:07, Kevin Vaughan, a local boy, finally came over the hill with the torch. The Brassfield Volunteer Fire Department and the South Granville Rescue Squad trucks set off their sirens and the folks strained to see.

Dan Hunt and a bunch of kids fell in running beside Kevin as they passed Margaret Jenkins' shady front yard where a goodly number had gathered. There was applause and cheers and the clicking of every camera in southeastern Granville County as Kevin made his way through the crowded intersection.

At 11:09, he handed the torch off to John Stallings, the mayor of Creedmoor, who, with his daughter Linda, 8, and son Kenneth, 10, had paid $75 for the honor. John, Linda and Kenneth ran with it for a bit, all of them holding on to it, and then handed it back to Kevin who disappeared down the road to Franklinton.

It had taken three minutes, from first glimpse to last view, and as Kevin headed on down highway 56, some folks started singing "God Bless America." There were goose bumps on a lot of arms.

It was over at 11:10 and they took down the flags in just a few minutes. Then some folks went to Lena Gooch's house, where she fed them all vegetable soup.

Beverly Lunsford from Hillsborough was wiping tears the whole time.

"It was beautiful," she said.

Yes, it truly was.

On the Cold Edge of Life

He was out on the cold, dark edge of life, out where time seems to stop, out where you feel your body dying and there is nothing you can do about it.

Scant inches away from where he lay — broken, bleeding and freezing to death — rush-hour commuters and Christmas shoppers sped past, hurrying toward warm homes and gaily decorated stores.

Maybe the drivers didn't see him at all. Maybe they thought they saw something in the flash of headlights but dismissed it as a roadside pile of trash or a dead animal. Maybe they were just too busy to go back and check. The thought is awful, but maybe someone did see him and didn't want to get involved, so they left him to die.

"I knew if I went to sleep, I'd die," Joseph Balint Jr. said. "I was blind from the blood in my eyes, so I kept awake by counting the sound of cars going by. I remember counting 900 of them."

Joe became more than just another victim of a traffic accident that holiday season a decade ago. His lonely suffering became a symbol of a society grown cold, a society that turned its back on a stranger in trouble. The story of what happened that night brought unwanted worldwide attention to Raleigh. But the symbolism was wrong, Joe says, and after 10 years he wants to set the record straight.

He was 23 then, a young man hurrying home from his welding job at 5:30 p.m. on the night of Dec. 4, 1975. His wife Teresa had dinner waiting for him. He was riding his motorcycle on a shortcut trail beside railroad tracks just east of Old Wake Forest Road, where Atlantic Avenue is now. He had traveled it many times before the accident happened.

"I only have flashes of memory of what happened that night," he said. "I was going along the trail about 50 miles an hour when the next thing I knew I was eating ground. Nothing hurt then, and I just hoped I hadn't damaged the bike. I figured I'd better get up and get going because dinner was waiting.

"I decided to move and nothing happened. I couldn't move. I knew then I was hurt pretty badly."

He didn't know how badly he was hurt. Starting at the bottom, his left foot had 12 broken bones, his left leg was broken in two places, his pelvis was broken and his left hip was dislocated. His left arm had a compound fracture and was bleeding. Both wrists and both hands were broken and a thumb was crushed and bleeding. Both shoulders were dislocated. His nose and his jaw were broken, and he had lost four teeth. He was losing a lot of blood. The temperature was in the 20s and falling fast. He was in a deserted field where he might not be found for days. It had grown very dark.

"I decided I couldn't stay there," he said. "People have died from shock and exposure trying to decide what to do.

"I found that I could move my right leg, so I started pushing myself with my leg and steering with my head."

He pushed himself along, inch by agonizing inch, trying to make it to the Raleigh Beltline where he knew someone would stop to help him. The Beltline and the safety it promised were a long 800 feet away.

It took an hour to reach the bottom of the steep highway embankment, and then he began the long, slow climb up the hill. He reached the halfway point and found himself on a small access road. The Beltline was 25 feet away, up a 45-degree embankment. There was a small gully a few inches wide that ran up the embankment and he used it like a ladder, pushing himself along on his back with his one good leg.

His tortuous journey to what he thought would be his rescue took two hours.

"I wasn't really hurting," he said. "It was very cold and I think the cold is what kept me from hurting so much. It only hurt when I tried to move something that was broken.

"I came up in the median between the two traffic lanes. That was as far as I could get. It was about 7:30 by then, and I assumed somebody would stop to help me as soon as I got to the road. I got as close to the pavement as I could get and propped myself up on my helmet facing traffic.

"I tried to wave at cars but I couldn't move my arms. I tried to take off my helmet and throw it at a car but I couldn't get it off because my arms didn't work. I had gone temporarily blind from the blood in my eyes. So I just there facing traffic, waiting for someone to stop.

"After the first dozen cars went by without stopping, I got scared."

Joe Balint lay by the side of the Raleigh Beltline — his broken, bleeding body actually touching the pavement — for three hours while hundreds of people drove by him without stopping.

No one knows how many people drove by him that cold night without stoping. Joe was afraid that if he fell asleep or passed out he would die from blood loss and exposure, so he kept himself awake by counting the sound of cars going. He thinks he reached 900 before he heard the sound he had been waiting for.

"I heard a Volkswagen," he said. "You can always tell those. I heard it go by, stop and back up. Then I heard voices.

"I told them not to touch me, just to call the police. The guy had a citizens band radio in his car, and it seems like the police were there in a minute.

"It was so warm in the ambulance. I had been cold for so long and it felt so warm in there. But then, when I got warm, the pain started. I couldn't believe how much I hurt."

Five hours had passed since Joe had gone down on his bike. The first two hours had been spent dragging himself to the highway and he had lain there for three hours waiting for someone, anyone, to stop. But no one did until the man in the Volkswagen came by.

The story of what happened the night of Dec. 4, 1975, made Joe famous. The story of how an injured Raleigh man was ignored was printed and reprinted across the United States. He received sympathetic mail from all over the nation and several other countries.

"The whole tone of the stories and the mail I got was that society didn't care anymore," he said. "But I never felt that way. I was never angry at all. I was proud to have survived it. I wasn't angry that 900 people didn't stop, I was grateful that one did.

"I was wearing dark clothes that night, and where I was lying I would have been visible for only a few seconds. I'm sure a lot of people saw something that night but figured it was a bag of garbage or a dog. If they thought they had seen something, they would have had to make quite an effort to get off the Beltline and come back around to see what is was. I had my white helmet on, but my head was right on the white line so I probably blended in.

Later, I could understand why they didn't see me.

"I didn't hold anything against anyone then, and I don't now. People said society didn't care, that people were cold and cruel, but that's not so. Hundreds of people helped me then and now. There is no short supply of people who are good, kind and caring."

The doctors told Joe he would be in the hospital for months and would never walk unaided again. He proved them wrong and left the hospital after 15 days. He was back at work within four months and back on his motorcycle in five.

"The accident turned out to be a good thing," he said. "I was 23 then, a young 23-year-old who acted 18. I suddenly realized I was mortal. I had the classic midlife crisis at 23. I knew then I had to do something with my life. I had dropped out of college and had said I would go back, but you can count on your fingers the number who do go back. I made plans then to go back and get my degree."

It took another four years for Joe to go back to college, and it took him six more years to finish as he worked his way through.

But he did it.

"A lot of people think they can do extraordinary things, but very few people get the chance to prove it," Joe said. "I did. I survived. I don't have to apologize for being here. I worked very hard for it. And I have a debt to society I can never repay.

"When I see something on the side of the road I can't identify, I stop and go back. It is never more than a bag of garbage, but you never know."

Bound by a Paper Chain

Four Oaks

Butch Baker said: "I don't know what it's good for. I've just got it."

Butch's wife, Geraldine, never one too shy to add her two cents worth, chimed in: "I don't want it, either, but I've got it."

"IT" sits beside Butch's chair in their country home outside Four Oaks. "IT" is coiled in a pile 4½ feet wide, 3 feet high, and if "IT" was stretched out all the way, "IT" would reach from Butch's easy chair to Thornton's Lunch in downtown Four Oaks, and that is about four miles away.

"IT" is a paper chain, one of those things children make. They take gum wrappers, fold them in strips and weave them together in a chain. Then they throw them away.

But not Butch. It was Feb. 18, 1979. You may remember it as the day it snowed all day. It was Butch's birthday, he was snowed in and he was bored silly.

"I picked up a pair of scissors and started twirling them around," he said. "I began to think about girls who made paper chains and I started cutting pieces of paper and linking them together. It looked like a pretty good thing so I kept at it."

That might be the understatement of the year. Yeah, he kept at it all right. That paper chain begun on a snowy Sunday afternoon in 1979 has taken over Butch's life and his living room. And it just about killed Geraldine last week.

"I had to move it so we could get some new carpet put in," she said. "It took me and a girlfriend two days to move it. It was piled higher than my head. I was so sore the next day I couldn't move. I'd like to drag it out in the yard and set fire to it, I really would. He's got it bad."

"I'm not the kind of person to be doing something like this," Butch admits. "But the longest I've ever gone without working on it is a month. And I'll tell you the truth, I was miserable."

Consider this: It takes 147,840 strips of paper to make one mile of that chain and it is now almost four miles long. That is a lot of sitting and cutting.

"I've worn out four pair of scissors," Butch lamented. "My elbow got so sore I had to go to the doctor. I've got callouses on my fingers from the scissors. It's like a disease."

Still he sits there doing it. His idea of a good time is a Sunday afternoon, sitting in his chair, watching a ball game on TV, listening to a stock car race on the radio, listening to his police scanner and making his chain.

The biggest problem is finding what Butch calls "quality paper."

"The brochures that car dealers put out are real good," he said. "But they look at me funny when I get four or five for the same kind of car."

Geraldine said she's gotten her share of funny looks, too. "Any time we go somewhere, we get all the tourist brochures they put in those racks. I even go to truck stops to get them. That's not shoplifting, is it?

"Any time we check into a motel, he just sits there cutting up brochures, so the thing is always with us. If somebody sends me a card at Christmas that I want to keep for sentimental reasons, I have to hide it to keep him from cutting it up for that chain."

Geraldine's bark is worse than her bite. After all, they've been married for 25 years and she's used to Butch's odd ways. "He was all hepped up over pot holders at one time. I had pot holders up to my elbows. Finally I said, 'Butch, I've got enough pot holders!' I'll tell you, a lot of women would not have put up with it.

"One day the chain got tangled up in my vacuum cleaner and I had to tear it apart to fix it. But I don't say anything any more. He could be out running around with women in some beer joint. At least I know where he is, sitting there watching television and working on that chain."

Folks like to come see Butch's chain. They are all welcome but Geraldine grumbles that if they keep coming, she's going to start charging admission.

"I hear some of everything in the world when people see it," Butch said. "They say I'm crazy, and I say they're right. The fact is, I've got something that isn't worth a damn and no one wants it.

"But I wouldn't take a thousand dollars for it. And if I did, I'd start another one the next day. I've got something that no one else has and even if they started one today, they'd never catch up. I'd like to get it in the Guinness Book of World Records."

"I'll tell you one thing," Geraldine said. "I hope nothing ever happens to us, but if we got divorced, there would be no custody fight over the chain. He could have it.

"But you know, if he died, I couldn't bring myself to get rid of it. But I would load it in the back of his pickup truck and store it out of the house."

A Sanctuary for Animals

Scotland Neck

It is sunset on an early summer day. Bill Johnson is reared back in a rocking chair on the deck outside his log cabin that perches high on a bluff overlooking the Roanoke River. There is a goodly dollop of Old Forester bourbon in the glass beside him, a chaw of tobacco in his jaw and a view of a mile or more of the stately Roanoke in front of him.

On the other three sides of his cabin are 300 acres of his very own wildlife sanctuary, a sanctuary that teems with animals, including rare wild turkeys. No guns, no dogs and no trespassers are allowed. Nearby is a pond so full of fish they seem to want to jump into your frying pan.

"Some people have it made and don't know it," Bill said. "You're looking at one old boy who's got it made and knows it. But I worked like hell all my life so I could do this."

"You've got a little piece of paradise here," I tell him.

"You've got good sense, boy," he tells me.

Bill, as man and as boy, has been walking these woods, hunting this game and fishing these waters for most of his 66 years. He grew up and still lives in the house his mama and daddy brought him to when they moved from Raleigh 56 years ago. He has farmed some, made a few wise land investments and for the past 30 years was the forest ranger for Halifax County. And for all of that time, he has been his own man, doing it his own way.

"We had a new preacher in our church and I went to meet him," he said. "I told him, 'Preacher, I like to drink a little bourbon, I cuss sometimes, I like to play poker and I come to church when it suits me.' He said, 'It looks like I've got my work cut out for me.' "

And that he does. The man who tries to change Bill Johnson had better come prepared for a hard day's work.

But Bill himself admits that he's changed over the years. There is no man who loves the forest and all its creatures more than he does. For most of his life he has hunted, and the cabin walls are full of animals he's taken. There are stuffed deer heads and birds of all kinds and some imposing fish and snake skins and a wild turkey that takes your breath away with its beauty.

Bill still hunts, but he doesn't shoot as much as he used to. Now he's happy just looking and feeding and caring.

"I think more of the wildlife than I did before," he says. "I'm more interested in conservation now. I saw the way game was being taken, and I knew if it kept going like that there would be no more wild game for my children and grandchildren to enjoy. The idea of conservation began to appeal to me more. I enjoy seeing them as much as I do hunting them now."

Bill joined the forest service in 1955. He had applied to be a game protector, but when they told him he might have to leave his beloved Roanoke River valley, he politely turned them down and took the forest ranger job that would keep him here.

"I had my roots down here," he said. "I have loved that river from the first time I saw it."

He began building his private wildlife sanctuary 15 years ago when he bought the land he calls Sycamore Shores.

"Ever since I was a little kid I've wanted a log cabin," he said. "And when I got to be a big kid, I got a cabin."

He had a little better than 50 acres in his spread, and after he got the cabin built and the pond dammed up, he looked around and saw a bunch of woodland that belonged to Champion Paper Co.

"I wanted to build a place for the deer and the turkeys and the quail to come to where they would not get shot at," he said. "The only animal I ever shot here was a bobcat that broke into my wild turkey nest and killed all of them."

He rents the land from Champion and grows crops for the wildlife to eat. He has cleared land and trails and seeded it with wildlife food and corn for the animals.

And he is death on poachers. Some of the old boys in Halifax County, one of the most hunted counties in the state, like to spotlight deer from the roadside at night, and some of them like to float down the river and shoot what they see. But they have learned that if Bill Johnson, one of their own, sees them at it, he will turn them in.

Some of them have not taken kindly to his interference and have let it be known that telling on them could be dangerous. There were dark threats that his cabin might get shot up one night. Bill spits a glob of tobacco juice at the notion he might get hurt.

"As a forest ranger, I'm still a sworn law enforcement officer," he said. "I know how to take care of myself. I told the fellow who threatened me that I've been hunting, fishing and enjoying this Roanoke River for half a century, and if necessary I can be the baddest man on this river. I haven't had a bit of trouble since I told him that.

"I don't believe you should refrain from hunting. Wildlife is a crop and big business. We've had deer die by the hundreds because there was no food for them, but hunting needs to be managed and you have got to follow the rules."

We crawled onto his four-wheel mini-bike for a ride through his sanctuary. In 20 minutes we saw two wild turkey hens, one with young. It was a stirring sight that will forever convince me that Bill Johnson is right in what he has done.

Time for Nostalgia

I'm going to miss Piedmont Airlines.

It won't make any difference to most airline travelers, of course. The name on the tail of the aircraft in which you fly is of no real significance to anyone other than stockholders and employees. They all cost about the same to fly, and they all get you there most of the time.

To the folks at USAir who recently made a deal to buy Piedmont, it is solely a business decision. Piedmont has been a successful, profitable airline for several years, and it was prime pickings for the merger moguls and corporate raiders who buy and sell companies like you and I buy and sell cars. Somebody is going to make a lot of money and that's what it is all about.

But Piedmont represents more than a bottom line to the people of North Carolina. It is our airline. It is Air Carolina, if you will, our very own homegrown little puddle jumper that make it big.

Don't get me wrong. I have no stake in Piedmont. I don't own any stock in the company, and I don't know anyone who does. But I've flown Piedmont enough to make it my first choice. And when I fly it, it feels like I'm flying with home folks.

There was always a sense of coming home when I flew Piedmont. Coming back from overseas in the mid-1960s, I flew a variety of big airline jets including Northwest Orient, TWA, American and Delta to get to Atlanta, and then I crawled on a little rattling Piedmont propeller-driven plane and headed for

North Carolina. It was like catching a ride home with a neighbor.

I was traveling in uniform with several other guys and we were all heading for Raleigh on our way to our homes in Eastern North Carolina. There were not many people on the plane — unlike now when it seems that everybody is trying to get to Raleigh — and the stewardess, who had a brother in the war, took time to chat with us. She asked us all where we were from and when I told her I was from Wilson, we got to talking about mutual friends. I hadn't met anyone for a long time who even knew where Wilson was.

She was one of us, a pretty North Carolina girl with a sweet Southern accent, and as we flew above the dark Southern fields below, we knew we'd made it home even before the plane touched down. And that sweet thing served us free drinks all the way.

Piedmont brought airline travel to Eastern North Carolina when no one else would take the chance. Sure, we made fun of it. We called it Trans-Terrifying airways.

But while the big airlines were battling to get landing rights in New York, you could fly in and out of Goldsboro on Piedmont Airlines. I remember one flight from Fayetteville to Washington. Two of us soldiers were on a prisoner pickup assignment and as we took off from Fayetteville, the pilot said we'd be stopping at Goldsboro. I wasn't aware of an airport at Goldsboro and as we came in for a landing it was obvious that we were landing at Seymour Johnson Air Force Base. The little Piedmont plane landed in the midst of the giant war planes and taxied to a stop outside a mobile home that was the terminal.

You've just got to feel kindly toward an airline like that.

Piedmont has been the nice neighbor down the block who worked hard and made a success of himself, the kind of guy that everyone in town pulled for. And now our neighbor is leaving for the big city.

Piedmont's success has mirrored the success of North Carolina. It wasn't long ago that our state was just another sleepy Southern state and only home folks flew Piedmont. But North Carolina and Piedmont have hit it big in the last decade and, while I'm not a Wall Street business analyst, it seems that the two success stories must be related.

USAir says it has no plans at the present to change the name of Piedmont Airlines. They say it will be a wholly owned subsidiary with its own name and identity. But those in the know say that won't last — the best guess is that the name might change after a year or so — and one day we'll go out to the airport and there won't be a Piedmont anymore.

That won't make much difference to most people, I suspect. But it will to me.

Those of us who have had to live away from the South have all experienced the heart-warming joy of hearing a telephone operator with a Southern accent when we called home from whatever corner of the world we found ourselves in. It was the same with Piedmont. Other airlines flew anywhere you wanted to go, but for a long time, if a North Carolina boy or girl was flying home, they flew on Piedmont.

I'll miss that.

Sergeant Inspired His 'Gentlemen'

Sgt. Quinn must have choked on his beer when he heard the news.

I can see that pencil-thin mustache quivering, that lined and ruddy face turning a deeper red, those shoulders gathering closer to his neck, that Irish dander getting higher and higher.

He was, without any close competition, the toughest man I ever met. He would have gone into a rage when he heard about the umbrellas.

For a while, you see, the Army was considering allowing soldiers in uniform to carry umbrellas. The idea was canned.

Good thing. Sgt. Quinn would have gnawed his way through the stone walls of the Pentagon to express his displeasure, and no newspaper would have been able to print a word he said.

"My name is Quinn," he said the day we met. "But you can call me by my first name: Sergeant!"

It was Feb. 8, 1962. Sgt. Raymond Quinn was the platoon sergeant for the 3rd Platoon of Delta Company, 5th Battalion, 5th Training Regiment, Fort Jackson, S.C. I was a no-name private with three days in the Army.

He was short and skinny and hard. After eight weeks, I and the 80 other tigers from my barracks would have followed him into the gaping jaws of hell.

He was one of the old breed, a professional who wore his

uniform with pride, a man who loved his Army.

He was not a nine-to-fiver. He lived in a little room at the end of our barracks. His was the first voice we heard each morning and the last voice we heard at night.

Other drill sergeants seemed fond of sending their charges through the miseries of basic training while they stood around and watched. Not Quinn. His motto was that of the infantry: "Follow me."

Many were the dark mornings when he would roar into the barracks at 3 a.m. with a snootful of beer. You could hear his happy singing before he hit the front door, and it wasn't a bad voice. He'd stumble into his room and fall into bed.

Two hours later the lights would blaze on and there would be Sgt. Quinn, immaculate in starched fatigues and spit-shined boots, striding the floor and informing us we had five minutes to be in formation.

It was winter, and it was cold and dark at 5:05 a.m. We would line up, cold, tired, homesick and pitiful.

Sgt. Quinn would stand in front of us and smile. He would light a long cigar and say, "Gentlemen, let's take a little run."

Off we would stagger, in heavy uniforms and combat boots, for a two-mile run before breakfast.

Sgt. Quinn would be in front, talking and singing and puffing on his cigar while we ran. We were teenage boys in our prime, and he was a middle-aged man smoking a cigar while he ran backwards for the whole two miles.

He taught us that you take care of each other. If 80 men started, 80 men finished. If a man got sick or had a stitch in his side, you carried him. No one fell out.

The proudest moment I felt in the nine years I wore the uniform was because of Sgt. Quinn.

It was graduation day, the last day I would see him. There were a thousand graduating, and we were to march to a parade ground to pass in review and become soldiers. The parade ground was two miles from our barracks. It was all uphill.

We looked sharp. Sgt. Quinn taught us to not only perform as soldiers but to look sharp doing it.

Our platoon was the last in the long line. But Sgt. Quinn said we were the best, and it was our right to be first.

He lit the cigar and said the words: "Gentlemen, let's take a little run."

We passed the thousand, one man at a time, double-timing in a tight formation, every man in step, chanting as we ran up that long, long hill.

We passed the last man just as we arrived. In front of the assembled spectators and high brass, Quinn's Tigers ran onto that field in perfect step and came to a halt in front of the reviewing stand with sparkling precision and 80 grins.

I heard later that Sgt. Quinn got in trouble for his showboating.

He knew what he was doing. He had taken a ragged bunch of scared kids and in eight weeks had made them proud soldiers.

Sgt. Quinn must be retired by now. Wherever he is, I hope he's having the time of his life. And I'll bet he doesn't own an umbrella.

Mama's Mysterious Pocketbook

I know Mama must have had a lot of pocketbooks in her life — after all, she lived well into her 80's — but the only one I can remember was a shiny black patent-leather job with a gold-colored metal fastener at the top. Of course, it may have been that every pocketbook she owned was exactly alike.

Mama's pocketbook was an endless source of treasures for me. All the money I ever got came out of that pocketbook or to be more precise, from the little snap-top black silk change purse she kept inside it. She'd carefully dole out a quarter for the Saturday afternoon cowboy matinees or a nickel when the ice cream truck came through the neighborhood and I was about to die for a push-up.

Handkerchiefs came out of that pocketbook, too. Those small, lacy handkerchiefs that I used to buy her at Christmas because they were all I could afford or think of. Funny thing about those handkerchiefs: When I'd buy them they'd be all soft and feminine feeling, but when she'd pull one out, stretch it over her index finger, wet it with her tongue and attempt to scrub some offending smudge of dirt from my face in a public place, it seemed to be made out of high-grit sandpaper. It would almost take your skin off.

There we'd be, she holding the top of my head in a death grip, scrubbing on my scrunched-up face with that handkerchief, muttering about how boys can even get dirty in church, and me dancing around, whining and hoping against hope that none of my rough-and-tumble friends were within viewing distance.

My Mama's pocketbook — I never heard her call it a purse but I guess everyone does now — was a place of magic. I never once remember Mama reaching into that pocketbook and not finding what she was looking for. It seemed like a magician's coat sleeve. No matter what she wanted, it was in there somewhere.

She never searched for a safety pin without finding one. There was always a well-sharpened pencil — I shudder to admit that yes, I lived before everyone carried a ball point pen — and a little spiral notebook to write on. She kept stamps in there and what little makeup she wore. There was usually a small silver tin of her Sweet Lorillard snuff and a well-chewed black gum toothbrush to dip it with for those days when she went to call on her old lady friends.

But the thing I remember best about Mama's pocketbook was the smell of Beechnut chewing gum. My Mama must have chewed $10,000 worth of Beechnut chewing gum in her life. I never knew her to be without it. I'd get to fretting and she'd reach in, pull out a stick of spicy Beechnut and hand it to me. It worked.

Everything that came out of that pocketbook smelled of Beechnut chewing gum and it was a good smell. It was clean and fresh, and to this day, when I smell that smell, I think of Mama and that black patent-leather pocketbook.

But some of the time, I think of the day she caught me going through her pocketbook. It may have been one of my lowest days because I think she thought I was stealing from her.

For reasons lost in memory, I badly wanted a stick of chewing gum. I knew — just as sure as I knew that Roy Rogers would never lose a gunfight — that there was chewing gum in Mama's pocketbook. She wasn't in the house, but I was and so was her pocketbook.

It was lying on top of the white chenille bedspread that was the only bedspread I ever remember her having. I went in, opened her purse, found the chewing gum and then made a big mistake. I got interested in what else was in there.

To put it bluntly, I was nosy as only a small boy can be. I started idly pawing through the stuff in Mama's pocketbook. I don't think I'd ever seen the actual inside of the pocketbook she carried, and I was fascinated by this new world I had discovered. I do remember that I found a crumpled package of Lucky Strike cigarettes, and it was years later when I found out from an aunt that Mama used to enjoy a smoke from time to time. I naively assumed they belonged to someone else. My saintly Mama would never have smoked, or so I assumed.

I knew I was doing wrong because when I sensed I was not alone, my heart stopped. I looked up and there was Mama, standing in the doorway. I was holding her little silk purse at the time. I mumbled something about looking for chewing gum while holding her little bit of money in my hand, but I knew she didn't believe me. I know she thought I was stealing from her. It was in her face.

She didn't punish me. She was just very quiet for what seemed like forever. But I punished myself for both of us.

It was no big deal, but even now, 40 years later, I still get uncomfortable when I innocently look for something in my wife's purse. And I can't smell Beechnut chewing gum without thinking about Mama and her pocketbook.

Burning Leaves and Memories

I don't know who was older, the bent old man with the yard rake, the white frame house behind him or the strong old trees that were towering over both of them, but they'd all seen plenty of autumns.

The leaves on the tree and in the yard were bright gold, the brightest I've seen for years, and they were so fluffy that a waist-high pile of them wouldn't weigh a pound. It has been a good year for pretty leaves, and the old man in the yard seemed to be enjoying his autumn raking.

I'd stopped to take a break from driving, to stretch my legs, drink a Coke and eat a pack of Nabs at the country store that has been selling everything from snacks to mule harnesses and chewing tobacco to handkerchiefs (and giving away old memories and good conversation) for many generations.

I was out front, looking at the man across the road and sitting on a wooden bench that advertised Sunbeam bread. Most of the brightly colored paint had been rubbed away by years of serious loafing, but you could still see that smiling little girl. The ground in front of me almost seemed paved by the tens of thousands of bottle caps that had been thrown down and walked in over the years. This is the kind of place where folks still drink their drinks out of returnable bottles like God intended, not from plastic bottles where you can't feel how cold the drink inside is. And they don't drink from cans, either.

The old man kept working as I sat there watching him and thinking about not much at all. Then he did something I've missed doing for years and didn't even know it.

He reached into the back pocket of his bib overalls and came out with a big match. Not a book of matches or a lighter or even a penny box of matches. No, he pulled out an honest kitchen match, those strong, fat ones with the bulbous head. He struck it on the rake handle and it flared brightly. You could have seen it a mile away at night. He touched the match to the biggest pile of leaves and they caught right away.

He stood back as the smoke wafted up around his knees before leveling off and heading my way.

The leaves burned slow and easy, more bright orange glow than flame, and they filled the clear autumn air with a thin haze of blue-gray smoke.

The aroma reached me, and suddenly I was so homesick. I got a lump in my throat and moisture in my eyes, the way you get when your heart says you want to cry and your brain tells you that would be silly. You're a grown man, and grown men don't cry over burning leaves.

Yeah, sure we don't. And burning leaves on an autumn day in the country don't make us miss our dead mamas, either.

I've raked a lot of leaves in the past 25 years, and it has always seemed like work. But there was a time before then, when Mama and I would rake the yard on Saturday afternoons, when it didn't seem like work at all. It was fun then. I was with Mama, and I got to burn the leaves when the raking was over.

Burning the leaves was always my job. We'd rake the yard together and then Mama would go in the house and get a kitchen match. She'd stand there patiently while I lit the match, doing it just the way she told me, and watch as I'd bend over to touch the match to the leaves.

I always did a good job raking those leaves because the more leaves I had, the bigger the pile would be and the more fun it would be to burn them.

Mama would go sit on the front porch in that green porch chair of hers while I tended to the fire. I was a little boy, but I felt like a grown man doing it. Burning leaves was important work, and I took it very seriously. I made sure that the fire didn't spread and that it didn't go out, either.

After all, my Mama was depending on me and watching me,

and I wanted to do it right for her.

It was the smell that brought it all back, that smell of those burning leaves on an October afternoon.

Somebody decided, without asking me or you, that it was not good for those of us who live in town to burn our leaves anymore. I don't know why they did that, but we let them get away with it so it is as much our fault as theirs. They said it had something to do with pollution, but that's silly. Anybody who thinks the smell of burning leaves is pollution has lost touch with what is important. Diesel cars from Germany make pollution, not burning leaves.

They tell us we have to stuff our leaves in plastic bags now, and they'll come get them Wednesday. Or we can leave them by the road, and an ugly, noisy machine will come one day and suck them up a hose and take them away. Thanks a lot.

I hung around to watch the old man finish his good, important work. The last pile was almost gone when he walked across the road to the store to get a drink.

"Good day for burning leaves," I told him as he walked up.

He nodded but he didn't say anything.

"You know, they won't let us burn leaves in town anymore," I said.

He still didn't say anything, but he looked at me like I was crazy to live in a place that wouldn't let a man burn his own leaves in front of his own house on a sunny afternoon in late October.

He may have something there.

What Happened to Marbles?

There doesn't seem to be much marble shooting going on.

A low-tech boyhood game if there ever was one, marble shooting seems to have faded from the playgrounds like the echoes of recess after the class bell has rung. Perhaps the marble hustlers are still out there, drawing circles in the hard-packed ground and taking another patsy to the cleaners. Perhaps boys today do know what a hand span is and can lag to the line. Perhaps, but I haven't seen much of it.

I was never a good marble player. My role was to be the

supplier for those boys who were good. And some of them were very, very good.

We never played for funsies. It was for keeps every time. Only weenies and your little brother wanted to play for funsies, so an afternoon of marbles could set you back a dime or so.

We got our marbles at Edgar Norris' grocery store. They came in little bags, and you got about 10 for a dime. A serious marble shooter — and all of us thought we were serious — would inspect each bag to find just the right mix of colors and smoothness, the same way a grocery shopper would paw through bags of onions to find the right ones.

Perfect grassy lawns and paved streets might have something to do with the death of marbles. What you needed was a hard-packed dirt yard, smooth and free of tree roots. Callas Bridgers, my next-door neighbor, had the perfect yard for marbles. There was not a blade of grass in the back, and they had a big shady tree.

We played two games. For one of them, we drew a circle about 3 feet across and placed our stake of marbles in the middle. It was sort of like the ante in poker. We'd decide, based on how many players there were and how many marbles each of us had, how many to risk. With four players, we'd ante about three marbles each and place then all packed tightly together in the middle of the circle. Then we'd draw a small circle around that pack.

Lagging to the line started the game. We'd draw a straight line about 10 feet away and toss our shooters toward the line. The closest to the line won the right to go first.

Serious marble players would kneel at the edge of the circle and place their middle knuckle on the line. "Knucks down" was the cry if someone tried to put their first knuckle down. The worst thing you could do was fudge. Fudging was when you tried to sneak your knuckle an inch or so inside the line before shooting. I've seen fearsome wrestling matches start over that small violation, because if the word got out that you were a fudger, well, your standing in the neighborhood was shot.

Beginners, weenies and little brothers were allowed a hand span handicap. They could place their thumb on the line and draw an arc with their outstretched fingers and shoot from there. It was a sissy thing, but if it was allowed, you took it. Then the game began. You shot untill you knocked a marble out of the big circle. It was yours to keep.

The rules were cruel. If you tried to shoot a marble out of the little inner circle and left your shooter inside it, your shooter became part of the pot. Ricochets were the idea — knock one out and get your shooter out,too.

It could go on for hours and when the last marble was knocked out, you counted up your take and either went home and moped or tried again. The good marble shooters could take every marble on the block before dark.

A more vicious game was played with a triangle instead of a circle. You placed the marbles in a triangle drawn on the ground and started shooting from the lag line and kept shooting from wherever you happened to be in the yard. You forfeited your shooter any time you stuck it inside that triangle.

The big boys, like 13 or 14, thought they were too cool to play marbles. Those jerks used to step on our marbles and mash them into the dirt. That was mean because a marble that has been scratched with dirt is no good as a shooter. It sticks to your thumbnail when you try to shoot.

Marble playing did not make better boys of us. It quickly introduced us to the concept of gambling — a marble dropped on a school room floor was guaranteed to get all of your marbles confiscated by a teacher (what did they do with the thousands of marbles they confiscated in elementary school?), and the next logical step up from marbles was shooting pool. And we know where that leads, don't we? Girls.

I hope there are boys playing marbles. (No sexism intended, but I never saw a girl who could shoot marbles worth a flip.) It would reassure me there is hope for the Laser Tag set.

Who Says It's an Eyesore?

The three-page document was chock-full of whereases and good intentions. But if its intentions are realized, rural North Carolina is going to have as much down-home flavor as instant red-eye gravy.

It was called House Resolution 1035, but the title was a bit misleading: "A House resolution honoring the life and memory of Mrs. Eugenia Patterson VanLandingham and thereby applauding the efforts to remove or improve abandoned structures which blight the scenic beauty of North Carolina's roadways."

What the last part means is that some well-intentioned people want to improve our image by getting rid of those dilapidated tobacco barns, sagging tenant houses, abandoned country stores, lonely chimney sentinels and other architectural remnants of our past that grace our rural roads.

Not so fast, folks. These are our roots you're ripping up and burning down.

HR 1035 was introduced into the General Assembly by Rep. Josephus L. Mavretic of Tarboro and was adopted June 6, 1985. In part, it pays tribute to Eugenia VanLandingham, a great lady who died a few years ago after serving many years as a home economics extension agent in Edgecombe County.

Now, I have no quarrel with the decision by the N.C. Extension Homemakers Association and the Eastern N.C. Chamber of Commerce to honor Mrs. VanLandingham by dedicating this "Remove-Improve" campaign to her memory.

But the rest of HR 1035 is something else. Strip away the legalese and it says, "North Carolina . . . has developed over more than four centuries an agrarian society . . . (and) a farm-tenant network that has long since been abandoned.

"Left behind from yesteryear, there are tenant houses, no-longer-used farm buildings and other structures that are falling into unused decay along the most extensive highway system in the nation.

"While seeing a few of these abandoned and decaying structures may provide a feeling of nostalgia to visiting passers-by, seeing one after another could create a feeling of decay, and a lack of community and state pride."

It goes on, but you get the idea: The old homeplace, unless you can fix it up or unless it has historical significance, should be torn down and hauled away.

The purpose of this voluntary effort to clean up our roadsides, the resolution concludes, is "to improve the appearance of our great State and to present it in an improved light to tourists, to industrial prospects and to its own citizenry."

It makes a man want to cry.

There is one of those abandoned houses in the Sandy Cross community of Nash County. It is a shabby eyesore, but my daddy grew up there. Sometimes when I'm in the neighborhood, I stop by and watch the old place and imagine a little Earl Rogers running around that dirt yard in his droopy diapers. It makes me feel close to a man I didn't know very well. I like to do that and I'll do it as long as one board is left. Please spare that falling-in shack while you're sprucing up for the tourists.

There is another dilapidated house covered in vines and undergrowth on a side road near Cherry Grove in Columbus County. It was there an old-time, bonnet-wearing, country grandma used to let me sit with her on the screened-in back porch while she churned butter by hand and I watched in wide-eyed wonder.

It may be that out-of-staters will look at our falling-down tobacco barns in the fields, think we're rubes and take their factories somewhere else. It may be that some people would prefer to see a vacant lot at a crossroads instead of an abandoned general store with peeling paint and a Sinclair dinosaur sign holding it together.

But one man's eyesore — some windowless tenant house covered in kudzu — is someone else's ancestral home. A lot of us didn't have relatives in the big houses with historical significance that are deemed worth preserving.

Our folks were the tenant farmers and the poor people who lived in the old shacks the Chamber of Commerce folks want to tear down to make the roadside more pleasant for the factory builders and the tourists. Our folks sweated in those tumbledown barns and bought their meager groceries in those sagging general stores.

The civic leaders are right. The old places aren't much to look at, and they sure aren't worth fixing up. But they are part of who we are and who we were.

And I'm very sorry if my daddy's old house is embarrassing to anyone, but places like that mean a great deal to a lot of us. Time and the wind will take the old places away soon enough, and that is the way it should be.

But please, not a bulldozer.

A Remembrance of Gad

The old man would have no more left the house without his pocketknife than he would have gone out without his battered old felt hat and his knee-high rubber boots. He would have felt naked without them.

It was a small knife, maybe three inches long with a two-inch blade. The handle of stag horn, worn smooth over the decades.

He'd had the knife as long as I'd known him.

He would sit there in his green chair after supper, listening to Gabriel Heater on the radio, and slowly sharpen his knife on a little whetstone worn thin in the middle. A haze of Prince Albert pipe tobacco smoke would fill the room.

There would be no talking in the room. No one spoke while Gabriel Heater was on the radio. And you didn't stand in front of the radio, either. Gad wanted a clear view of the old Philco table model when he listened.

His name was Issac Thomas Lamm, but I called him Gad for reasons lost in family mythology. Officially, he was my step-grandfather, but the "step" part didn't seem to be all that important. He was Gad, my grandfather.

Gad was not one of those fat, warm, cuddly old grandfathers with a cherubic smile who bounced laughing grandchildren on his knee. He was tall and ramrod straight and didn't talk or smile very much. His days had been hard ones, and he had no use for frivolity. He was a 19th-century man lost in the 20th.

We were inseparable.

He was the only man I ever knew who farmed inside the town of Wilson. We lived in the Five Points area, and at the end of Aycock Street, down the hill by the creek, Gad raised collards for a living.

We were a familiar sight around Wilson. Each morning during the collard season he and I would go down to the collards, and he would harvest a wagon load. It was about 1950, but Gad still drove a mule and wagon an the streets of our town. He'd load the wagon and we'd head off behind his mule.

I can only imagine what people thought of us, the old man and the scrawny kid perched up on that wagon looking so out of place. Gad probably was considered an eccentric old coot because ours was the only wagon I ever saw on the streets of Wilson. This was, after all, 1950, and cars were everywhere.

But there we went, slowly plodding along our way, oblivious to the 20th century. We'd call on stores all over town, many of them neighborhood stores. By noon we'd be empty and heading home, a few dollars in his pocket and the best, freshest collards in town heading for Wilson's supper tables that night. And I would be full of snacks handed out by the good people who ran those little neighborhood groceries.

Along about that time Gad decided he wanted to build us a new house. But he wanted to do it his way; no contractors or blueprints for him.

He chose a small lot at the corner of Crawford and Aycock streets and went to work. He made a machine out of wood to form the cement blocks he wanted. He mixed up the cement (hauled to the site with his mule and wagon) in a wooden trough he'd made himself and shoveled the mix into his rude, homemade mold. Day after day, he'd pour a batch of blocks and set them out to dry in the sun. Once he had enough blocks made, he dug a foundation with a shovel and laid every block himself.

The only thing he hired to be done was the plumbing and wiring. And when he roofed it and covered it with stucco and we moved in, he looked at it and liked what he saw.

So he did it all over again, from scratch, next door.

He was about 80 years old when he finished, and the second house was better than the first. Both still stand in Wilson.

Gad died in the late 1950s. It was in the middle of the night, and he went gently in his own bed.

I had not thought of Gad in a long time until last week when an acquaintance from Wilson started telling me about this old town character he used to see on the streets with his mule and his wagon and his collards and a scrawny little boy who followed him everywhere.

"Did you ever see him?" he asked. "He would have made a great column."

Mules Make for Disaster

The Army has lost its mind.

Full-tilt crazy is the only explanation for an announcement that the Army is considering using mules as pack animals.

Who am I to be telling the Army what it should do? I am a survivor of a mule, that's who. I know those miserable, four-legged creatures far too well.

I don't want to hear any grief about cruelty to animals for what I am about to tell you. I tried my best to kill a mule, and I regret that I failed.

I was 10 years old, and we were putting in tobacco. My job, my first, was to drive a mule-drawn sled through the field while the croppers loaded it with tobacco and then to drive it to the barn.

The croppers began their slow walk down the rows. I picked up the reins and slapped the mule's back like they did on stage coaches.

It did not work. I hit a little harder. I yelled "giddy up" in my squeaky little voice, which made everybody laugh.

The croppers were way down the row and their arms were full; they were beginning to growl. I was the boss's grandson, so, automatically, I was the village idiot. And I felt like it.

One of the croppers came back to the drag where I was on the verge of tears. He picked up a tobacco stalk and hit the mule.

The mule leaped forward, dumping me on my skinny little bottom, and took off down the row. I jumped up screaming "whoa" and chasing the mule.

The croppers, those that had not become convulsed with laughter, stopped the mule.

It was my turn. They had shown me how. I never said a word. I got in the drag and swung a tobacco stalk at the mule's behind like Joe DiMaggio at the plate.

The mule turned around, looked at me and took off down that row at full gallop, which was not a pretty sight because nothing runs worse than a mule.

I still had the reins, so I leaned back as hard as I could and yelled "whoa" as loud as I could. What we had was an 80-pound kid going one-on-one with a 600-pound mule.

The croppers saw us coming. They did not try to help. They threw tobacco every which way and dove for safety. We blew down that row, the drag careening from side to side, stalks slapping me in the face, me yelling, and the mule going crazy.

I had heard something about "gee" and "haw," so I tried that. He took one step to the side and suddenly we were straddling a row, ripping up about a million dollars worth of prime tobacco, or so Daddy claimed.

The woods were dead ahead. On we charged, me and the mule and the bouncing drag with devastation in our wake.

That sure-footed mule took a 90-degree turn at full gallop, and if we had not hit a tree the drag would have turned over and thrown me out. That would have been good.

But what happened was the drag bounced off the tree, and the mule kept on going to the path that led to the mule barn.

I figured the worst was over, but I was wrong. The mule slowed but would not stop, no matter what I did. Mules are cruel to 10-year-old boys.

The path to the mule barn went by the tobacco barn where 30

people were working. They thought I was coming in with a load.

We kept right on going. The mule was calmly plodding along with me in the drag crying, scared, embarrassed and screaming "whoa."

They thought that was the funniest thing they had ever seen. They fell in behind us as we headed to the barn.

The mule walked into the pasture as calm as could be, went over to the trough and started drinking water.

I was crazed. I grabbed a limb and proceeded to beat that mule to death.

Did it hurt the mule? Of course not, I'm sorry to say. He never looked back. He just kept on drinking and occasionally switching his tail.

Then the rotten beast did something I'll never forgive.

A little girl picked up the reins and made a funny noise with her mouth. The mule sedately headed back to the field like a docile puppy, where she handled him for the rest of the day with ease.

I had to stay at the barn and do her job. Me, a boy, having to do a girl's job.

I never forgave the mule. Or that girl.

Don't do it, Army. You'll be sorry.

Rose-colored Memories

We had fire drills in school where we joined hands and marched outside. We had tornado drills where we sat in the hall with our backs to the wall and our arms over our heads. The drills could have saved our lives in an emergency.

There was another drill that wouldn't have helped a bit, but it didn't feel useless.

The teacher would yell "Flash!" and we'd get under our desks.

Why did we think a half-inch of wooden desk top would keep the nuclear holocaust outside our classroom windows? But we had to do something, didn't we? It wasn't the American way to sit there and fry. We used to laugh and play as we went outside for a fire drill. No one snickered as we huddled under those desks. Fire didn't scare us. Atomic bombs did.

The hottest movie one recent year was a pleasant little flick called "Back to the Future." It is about a boy who goes back 30 years, back to 1955 when his parents were the age he is now. It is light-hearted entertainment that perpetuates the gentle "Myth of the Fifties."

It was the decade that invented rock 'n' roll, flat-top haircuts, pop-top beer cans, poodle skirts and Davy Crockett hats. But it was also the decade when dealers sold do-it-yourself backyard bomb shelters and made good money doing it.

We had eight years of good old Ike in the '50s, that balding, grandfatherly president whose golf score at Burning Tree was the subject of national discussion. He also sent Marines to Lebanon and the Army to Vietnam.

But that is not the way the '50s are remembered. We use the word "turbulent" when we mention the '60s, but the '50s linger as 10 years of placid, happy, mist-shrouded days. The '60s had a harsh press, but the nation still has a love affair with the '50s.

We have AIDS in the '80s. In the '50s it was polio. In North Carolina, public swimming pools and movie theaters were closed one hot summer because of the polio scare. The national panic then was far worse than the AIDS crisis of today. How scared we kids were and relieved our parents were when we lined up at school to take those life-saving shots that Jonas Salk had said would keep us out of those huge, terrifying Iron Lungs.

The '60s and early '70s had the Vietnam War with attendant political drama. The '50s began with a similarly divisive Korean War that led to the public firing of a popular general, Douglas MacArthur, whose dismissal was followed by the largest ticker-tape parade New York had ever thrown for a returning hero. Many people did not like Richard Nixon, but almost nobody liked Harry Truman. Truman fired MacArthur for failing to support American policy, but it was MacArthur who ended up addressing Congress.

We are concerned with Russian missile deployment in the 1980s, and in the 1960s we almost went to war over missiles in Cuba. But in 1957, an unarmed basketball-sized sphere with antennae protruding from it scared us far worse. It was obvious to the man on the street and the kid in the playground that if the Russians could launch Sputnik, they could launch an atomic bomb over our heads. We sat by our radios listening to the "beep-beep-beep" as that unseen but deeply felt satellite moved across American skies seven times a day.

But memory revels instead in juke boxes with bubble lights; virgin pins and ponytails; white socks, rolled-up jeans and loafers; panhead Harleys, hot rods and '57 Chevy tailfins; Our

Miss Brooks and that pea pickin' Tennessee Ernie Ford and Sgt. Bilko; a rock 'n' roll madman named Alan Freed on the radio and Buddy Holly.

Maybe it is just as well we don't clearly remember Sen. Joseph McCarthy with his "I have a list . . . " or Julius and Ethel Rosenberg or Little Rock when paratroopers with loaded weapons faced off against National Guardsmen and waited to see who would twitch.

We who grew up then have children now and maybe they won't remember much about Vietnam or Memphis or Dallas or Silver Spring or Watergate.

Maybe someday the '60s will be granted innocence, too, just like the '50s have been.

Time and memory are anxious to forgive.

Big Lies by Big Folks

It was just awful the way the grown-ups used to tell bodacious lies to us dumb, trusting younguns.

I would hope, in these enlightened days, that this stuff does not go on anymore, but when I was a kid the lies they told us were so outrageous that us pint-sized yard apes had no choice but to believe them. Most of them were matters of life and death.

I'm not talking about your folk myths. You've got your Easter Bunny scam and that Tooth Fairy jazz but that was different. We knew there was nothing to that mess, but we got candy at Easter and a dime when we lost a tooth, so we were not about to blow a good thing. Anyone who wants to put a $5 bill (inflation, you know) under my pillow after a trip to the dentist is still welcome to do it. Hey, we younguns were dumb, but we weren't stupid.

I'm talking about the Big Lies that scared us so bad we believed them with all our innocent little hearts. We're talking the dreaded Poison Milk.

There were only a few things that were gospel during the time I was growing up on that black dirt tobacco farm near Cherry Grove in Columbus County: God would strike you dead where you sat if you played "Between the Sheets" during preaching at the Cherry Grove Missionary Baptist Church, and if you drank milk with fish you would get sick and die.

I'm not lying to you; if you drank a big glass of milk with a plate of fried fish, you were a goner.

The way I figured it out, there was some weird chemical reaction between milk and fish that turned the milk to poison as soon as you swallowed it. I don't know why we were told that, but it was the law of the land. You drank iced tea with fish, or you went thirsty. There was no known antidote, either. The first time I ever saw anyone eat oyster stew, I just knew they were committing suicide.

Drinking milk and eating fish was almost as dangerous as getting bitten by a turtle.

You let a turtle grab hold of you, and the turtle would hang on until it thundered. God help you if you were in the middle of a drought. I had scary visions of spending weeks during a dry spell walking around with a turtle dangling from my body.

What really scared me was that I had never seen much in the way of ears on a turtle. I was scared that even if one bit me on a stormy August afternoon he wouldn't hear it thunder even if there did come up a storm.

This turtle and thunder business put a definite crimp in our skinny-dipping. Turtles still are not among my favorite of God's creatures.

You were not even safe if you stayed away from turtles in the swamp because no one could escape the dreaded hoop snake. You could outrun a turtle if you saw him in time, but when the hoop snake got after you . . . well, it is all too sad to think about a child struck down like that.

The hoop snake was a snake about 5 feet long that would grab its tail in its mouth and go rolling across the fields like a Hula-Hoop. This guy was fast. No one could outrun it.

What it did was build up speed until it reached the target. Then it would let go of its tail and launch itself right at your behind like a spear. It was a terrible way to die.

We were dog-loving country folks. Everybody had dogs — some had dogs that would actually suck eggs — but no one had a cat. There were a few barn cats, but nobody played with them much, and nobody let them in the house.

The reason was simple. If you left a cat alone with a baby for even a minute, that cat would jump up on that innocent baby and suck the breath right out of its precious little mouth.

You weren't even safe when you were asleep in your bed because your dreams could be fatal. You could dream about monsters and people chasing you and finding yourself standing buck naked in a public place and that was fine, but if you dreamed you were falling, and you didn't wake up before you hit the ground, well, it was nice to know you.

And may the Good Lord have mercy on the people who walked in their sleep. It was a known fact that if you caught someone sleep walking and woke them up, they would drop dead at your feet.

I won't even go into what happened if you kissed your own elbow.

Demise of the Front Porch

I go by the old house on Briggs Street in Wilson every chance I get. I used to live there, and I used to sit on that big front porch. Mama would shell peas and try to get me to help her. I would until the green stuff packed under my thumb nail and it got sore and then she'd accuse me of throwing away more peas than I was shelling so I'd quit.

I hated shelling peas, but I loved that front porch. Even when it was hot, there would be a breeze stirring.

But then they started giving neighborhoods names and building what they called ranch-style houses and that was pretty much the end of front porches and civilized life. The names they gave the neighborhoods usually referred to what they destroyed to build them. And I have been on some real ranches and the houses never looked like ranch-style houses. And they all had front porches.

There haven't been many front porches built in the last 50 years. They were replaced by a little spot of concrete and some steps. These stoops are big enough for one person to stand while knocking at the door. A party of two or more must decide who stands out in the rain. Even the person doing the knocking has to step off the porch when the front door opens.

It was the combination of air conditioning and television that killed front porches. House designers figured that no one was going to sit out there making polite conversation on a summer night when they could be inside in the cool watching someone talk for them.

There are few conversationalists who can compete with Johnny Carson. Talk of who just got married, the song of crickets and the gentle flicker of lightning bugs aren't enough when the A-Team blows up something.

Some people tried to overcome the dearth of front porches by moving everything to the back yard and calling it a patio. But sitting on a patio with friends is called "entertaining" and usually requires several days notice and some light refreshments. Front porch sitting is spontaneous and you don't have to do anything. You speak to whoever strolls by and you can decide if you want to invite them to sit for a spell. At most, you might offer some ice tea or, if you're that kind of person, a beer (although alcoholic beverages are best left to the patio).

Sitting on a front porch is do-it-yourself entertainment. You get back on the patio and everybody sits in a circle and looks at the host and expects to be entertained. People sit in a row on the front porch and silence is golden. You watch what's going on, who's going by and you talk about whatever comes up if anything does.

We didn't expect much from sitting on the front porch. Our entertainment demands were few. We didn't have to laugh every two or three minutes. No one had to come up with an amusing anecdote. We just sat there enjoying the evening and speaking when the spirit moved us. You entertain on patios and gossip on front porches.

Young folks used the front porch a lot to court. Unless it was real hot, the older folks would graciously go in the house at a reasonable hour, leaving the front porch free for some sweaty hand holding, awkward hugging and sneaky kissing. But the front window was left open so you didn't get carried away. The surest signal that it was time to pedal your bicycle on home was when the front porch light came on just as you started getting short of breath.

Crime was less in neighborhoods without names and with front porches. You dared not misbehave while walking down a street in front of houses loaded with sitters. You could run down the street buck naked in most neighborhoods these days and about the worst thing that would happen would be a stubbed toe.

Some new houses are coming complete with front porches but I never see anybody sitting on them. All I see are wreaths on every door and a few hanging plants but no people. They built them just for show, I think. I'm not sure they even know what front porches are for.

I'm buying a house now, and it does not have a front porch. It has a deck that looks out at nothing particularly interesting. For the moment, I'm still living in a house with a front porch and a swing and the world going by just for my personal enjoyment. I'm not sure I'm doing the right thing.

Dad's Foolproof Method

Now I don't mean to be ugly, but some kids are acting like monsters when they get in public. I'm not talking about your kids, but I'll bet you know the ones I'm talking about.

The older ones are cussing, dressing funny and running into people in shopping centers. The middle ones are running up and down aisles at movies. The little ones are screaming and grabbing things in the supermarket.

The reason for this nasty behavior is that apparently some folks don't know how to tell them to behave.

So what's new, you say? Adam and Eve had trouble communicating with their kids, too, you say.

What's new is that I have a solution. Actually, my daddy had the solution, but he's not around to pass it on, so I will. Somebody has to do it because we are sick and tired of your bratty young'uns.

Here is the solution. Take it to heart. Memorize it: You have to talk to kids in language they understand.

It doesn't do diddly-squat to say to a kid who is acting like a jerk: "I find your behavior intolerable and you must refrain or face retribution."

I heard something distressingly similar to that from a parent in a movie theater last week. Her cute little dickens had already knocked over two drinks and a box of popcorn, and that runs into some real money. The mood was ugly.

What that woman should have done was talk to her kid like daddy used to talk to me: "You move out of that seat again, young'un, and I'm going to jerk a knot in you."

I had seen knots in shoe laces, fishing lines and mule reins, and I did not want one jerked in me. Faced with a threat like that, I did not analyze exactly how he was going to jerk that knot — and especially not where he was going to jerk it — so I took him at his word and sat down.

It is simple. Children have wonderful, vivid imaginations, and you must use that against them. We're talking survival of the fittest, and adults are losing.

"You back talk me again, boy, and I'm going to stomp you into a mud hole and walk you dry" is another fatherly phrase I learned at dad's loving knee.

A kid knows about mud holes. He has stomped a few himself and he knows about that squishy stuff that comes up through your toes. That stuff could be him, and he knows it. Thinking along those lines makes a smart kid mind his manners.

"I'll wear you out" is a good all-purpose threat because it is so visual. Kids have worn-out sneakers and worn-out jeans. They have seen worn-out cars sitting in junkyards with no windows in them and weeds growing out of the hoods. Any kid with half a brain does not want to be worn out. They know it would be horrible, so they shape up.

I know some of you whose kids are at this very minute making life miserable for someone else are sitting out there being sensitive and saying I'm some kind of Neanderthal monster who advocates child abuse.

Wrong-o.

You're the ones abusing the little darlings by talking and nagging and whining them to death. I believe in good, clean threats a kid will understand.

The beauty of a threat like "If you don't sit down and behave yourself I'm going to tan your hide" is that you don't really have to do it. You threaten to withhold their computer privileges and you've got to go through with it or be seen as a wimp.

They know when you say something colorful and graphic such as, "You touch the paint job on my new car with your grubby little hands, young lady, and you'll draw a back a nub" that you're not really going to do it, but the picture in their little minds is so clear and unmistakable that they know you're serious.

Kids are a lot like mules. They'll get away with as much as they can and push you to the limit. But once you get their attention, they'll behave.

If you don't believe me, listen to your kids talk to each other: "Give me back my baseball, or I'm going to knock your head off."

They know what works on their own kind. Learn from them — or keep them at home where you can enjoy their antics.

Mama's Home Remedies

My mama was the best advertisement Vicks VapoRub ever had.

I don't care what it was, from a runny nose to double pneumonia, her cure was to cover the sick part with a heavy application of Vicks. She considered it a miracle salve, and before you were taken to Dr. Neeland, you spent a day or so smeared in Vicks. If the Vicks didn't cure you, you were "doctor sick."

I have to pause to tell you about Dr. Eugene C. Neeland. Every new doctor ought to be required to spend six months working with Neeland before being allowed to work on his own. They might not learn any new medicine, but they would learn a lot about taking care of sick people.

Neeland has been practicing medicine in Wilson (that's not quite right: Other doctors practice; Neeland does it right) for as long as I can remember. His office was in my neighborhood, Five Points, an area Wilson folks call a working-class neighborhood. That meant there were — and probably still are — a lot of honest, poor folks there.

Neeland was our doctor. He had one eye and a bad leg and was the kindest man I ever met. A lot of us Five Points people couldn't pay him all at once, and there is no telling how much money he never collected. He has spent his life taking care of poor folks. If there are doctors in heaven, he'll be chief of staff.

I just wanted to say that.

As much as we liked Neeland, Vicks VapoRub was our first line of defense against childhood colds. It worked for everything that was wrong above the waist. Got a stuffy nose? Take a marble-sized dollop of Vicks and jam it up the offending nostril as far as it would go. It smelled bad, stung your nose and made your eyes water, but it usually worked like Drano.

If that didn't work, you took a pot of boiling water, threw in a big dab of Vicks, put a towel over your head and bent over to inhale the fumes. I think the towel was there to keep the fumes from peeling the paint in the room.

Some people thought Vicks was at its best fighting chest colds. I'd get a little croupy and Mama would smear my narrow chest and back with about half a jar of the stuff. Then she'd heat a towel by holding it to the side of the coal stove in the living room and then wrap it around my upper body. I'd put on a flannel shirt and get into bed with so many covers that I couldn't keep my toes pointed up.

I would lie there and bake while those fumes did their job, usually all night.

I don't care how many baths you took, you and everything that touched you would reek of Vicks for a week.

Mama knew a lot about medicine. There is a medical condition known as looking a little peaked (pronounced "PEAK-ed"). The sure cure for that vague condition, sort of a bored, listless look, was iron tonic.

I don't know what that tonic was or its proper name, but it looked and tasted like you had dissolved a couple of hundred old galvanized roofing nails in mineral oil. It was a nasty gray color and had little grains of something dark and evil suspended in it. It came in very large bottles. I seemed to take a lot of it in the spring, and it worked.

"You're looking a little peaked," Mama would say, and before I could convince her I was fine, I'd have swallowed two tablespoons of that mess, and my mama had the biggest tablespoons in the world. Your jaw would crack just to get one in.

I might feel like 40 miles of bad road the next day, but I acted as frisky as a young colt just to keep from having to take any more tonic.

Iron tonic and Vicks were for mild maladies. The mustard plaster was for the big stuff. There were two kinds of mustard plasters, the kind Mama made from some stuff in the kitchen and the dreaded store-bought ones.

The homemade stuff was yellow like mustard. It would get smeared on your chest, where it would dry and "draw out the cold." It was merely smelly and messy, unlike the store-bought plaster that would scar you for life.

It was a rubberized thing that stuck to your chest like a foot-square Band-Aid. It didn't smell bad or hurt going on, but removing one was agony.

It came off in the morning. Mama would peel up one corner, and as I begged her to be slow and gentle, she would yank with all her might. My frail body would come up off the bed about six inches as I screamed.

I still don't have any hair on my chest and that is why.

It has been a long time since I smelled Vicks VapoRub, tasted iron tonic or had my chest ripped off by a mustard plaster.

But it hasn't been long enough.

Icebox, Young'uns and Davenports

I'm not talking about those quaint country sayings that my friend Roy Wilder in Spring Lake collects, stuff like: "He's so ugly his Mama had to tie a piece of bacon around his neck to get the dog to play with him."

I'm talking about normal, everyday stuff, like calling a sofa a davenport.

I don't know why we called it that then and I don't know why we don't now. We never called that long, padded thing in the living room a sofa or a couch. It was always a davenport, or if it was real short, a settee.

The words "love seat" were never mentioned in my house. They sounded a little risque. My dictionary says a davenport is a sofa that unfolds into a bed. Wrong. That's a sofa bed.

Take refrigerators. We never had one. We did have an icebox. It was a real icebox and the man came and brought ice from time to time. I had the job of emptying the drip pan. It was a messy and difficult task because the thing was wide, long, heavy and shallow. The water would start moving in small tidal waves and you'd have to run for the screen door because it was fixing to spill.

After we got rid of the icebox, we got a Kelvinator. I have no idea what brand it was because all big, white cold boxes were Kelvinators. Like all cellophane tape is Scotch tape no matter how much the 3-M company complains about it.

"The leftover chicken is in the Kelvinator," Mama would say late on Sunday afternoon just before we settled down to watch "Disneyland" on TV. It was a happy time of the week (and my life) — cold fried chicken and Tomorrowland.

People were called different things then. There were no elderly people or senior citizens or golden agers, there were just old people and we loved them. The bent old man down the street was known, not at all unkindly, as Old Man Barnes. His wife was Old Lady Barnes.

There were no children, kids, preteen, toddlers or any of those things. All minors, regardless of sex, were young'uns until they got big enough that the differences were noticeable. Then they became boys and girls.

Old Man Barnes used to ask, "Whose young'un are you?" every day I saw him. One day he said, "Whose boy are you?" and I felt as grown-up as I did the day I learned to whistle.

Take the word "poor." It was one of our favorite all-purpose words. It could mean you didn't have any money. It could mean sick, although then generally you said "poorly." It could mean pitiful. Or it could mean skinny.

My daddy was fond of saying of me, "That young'un eats so much it makes him poor to tote it."

Every national columnist from Miss Manners to Ann Landers has worried their pencils to a nub trying to come up with a euphemism for two unmarried people living together. "Sweet-mates" is one of the words they came up with. The Census Bureau came up with Persons of the Opposite Sex Sharing Living Quarters or "POSSLQs".

Not in Five Points, you didn't. It was called simply "shackin' up" and they were trashy.

Why did they change ear bobs to earrings? When I asked my buddy to let me play with his spy glasses, I didn't say binoculars. Any young'un who said binoculars was the kind of young'un that took baths voluntarily. We ate weenies in weenie rolls and soda crackers with our soup (usually crumbled and floating on top). Someone who said saltines probably threw rocks instead of chunkin' them: "Mama, he chunked me with a rock!"

Old people wore false teeth, not dentures. Women did not wear padded bras, they wore falsies and kept it a secret. They were not called comic books or even comics, they were called funny books or, in newspapers, funny papers.

Speaking of newspapers, now we have carriers. Then we had paperboys. And all shoes made of canvas were tennis shoes even if you played basketball in them.

Corn on the cob was "roasting ears" and you slurred it so it came out sounding like "rosinears." With it you drank sweet milk and loaf bread, unless you were eating seafood and then milk turned into poison and you would die if you mixed them. They never satisfactorily explained oyster stew to me, but I would never drink milk with seafood.

I still don't. You can't be too careful.

Big Saturday Night for GIs

They acted for all the world like characters from the John Wayne war movies they'd been weaned on.

There was the Italian kid who said he was from "Da City," taking for granted they knew which one. They called him Brooklyn. He was really from Queens, but they called him Brooklyn. He was big and slow-moving and a good partner to have on your side.

College Boy was from D.C. He'd done a year in college. But since the rest of them were, with luck, high school graduates, they looked to College Boy for intellectual leadership. He was also the best-looking, so if there was to be any chance of them picking up girls, he was it.

They called one kid the Runt. It was a cruel and unkind thing to say about a nice kid like Thompson, who was from the Midwest, but it was an entirely accurate description.

The fourth, and last of the lot was even runtier than Thompson, but ended up with the epithet of "Skinny." He was thin as a rail, a small-town boy on his own for the first time. They could have called him "Four Eyes," but they didn't, since three of the four wore glasses.

The luck of the alphabet brought them together. They all had joined the Army and ended up in the same basic training company at Fort Jackson, S.C., in the late winter of 1961-62. They were there to become trained killers in the service of their nation. The Army had its work cut out.

They ended up in the same platoon since their last names all came late in the alphabet. It turned out that they were to be even closer, since they all ended up on the same floor and same side and same end of the barracks. Folks have become friends with a lot less in common than they had.

They shared all the misery and the loneliness of the first few weeks of basic training. They got dirty and yelled at and soggy and hungry and tired and cold, and mostly they wanted to go home. But they got close. "Shared hardship" is what the psychologists call it. Army buddies is good enough.

So it was a good thing that they got their first weekend pass together. By God, they'd earned it. They were not great soldiers, but they were good ones. They did what they were told, kept their mouths shut and tried to stay in the middle of the pack so as not to be noticed. They had figured out how The System worked.

The pass was to be 24 hours of hedonistic orgy. Flat-out, first-class fun. Open the bars and turn loose the women of Columbia. Four trained killers are coming to town.

No one mentioned that the oldest of the lot was an aging 19. No one let it out that none of them had had so much as two beers in the same 24-hour period. No one mentioned that the wildest times any ever had was cutting fourth-period English. They were soldiers on pass with a myth to uphold.

They chose the Wade Hampton Hotel as their lair. They all chipped in, and College Boy rented a single room into which all four would sneak with the bevy of beauties they were sure to score.

It was about 3 p.m. Saturday by the time they got downtown. They had until noon Sunday, so they walked around for a couple of hours and then, choosing carefully, Brooklyn went into a liquor store and bought them a fifth of bourbon to share.

They took turns sneaking into the hotel until all four were safely inside the room. They figured they'd have a couple of drinks to get in the mood while they waited for the sun to go down and the women to come out.

The sun found them there the next morning, passed out around the room with more than half the bourbon untouched. Fatigue from four weeks of basic training, mixed with a little bourbon and a lot of inexperience had done them in. Their big night out, their first as soldiers, had begun and ended in a room in the Wade Hampton Hotel. And there, their first hangover had begun.

Demolition crews blew up the Wade Hampton Hotel in downtown Columbia at 7:58 a.m. one Sunday not too long ago. The kid they called Skinny saw the pictures and remembered that night years ago. He got on the phone to find Brooklyn, College Boy and the Runt to tell them about the hotel's demise and remember with them for awhile.

He had no luck. But he had to tell somebody, so he wrote a column about it.

Once Upon a Two-Stick Popsicle

The night bus to Raleigh was fast, cheap and efficient.

But I sure did miss those old SceniCruisers, those huge two-deck buses that were the rolling kings of the highway 25 years ago when more people rode the bus.

I was in Washington not long ago, fresh off a five-hour train ride north. It was time to head home, and I wanted to ride a bus again.

I used to ride a lot of buses, back in my '60s soldier days when a bus ride was the only way to get from an Army camp to a sweetheart's arms. Maybe that is what I remembered: the sweet expectation that made the trip a pleasure and the bus itself a friendly giant that took me comfortably home.

The buses still roll and still take soldiers home to sweethearts, but they have changed. The seats seem smaller, with less legroom, and the bus stations are sad places.

Buses have never been the fancy way to travel. Rich folks took the train, and in later years they flew. Buses were left to take people who didn't have money to places that didn't have trains.

The bus station in Washington is a modern, clean, well-lighted place that is efficiently devoid of personality. It could be anywhere from Tampa to Tucson. It has no sense of place. The terminal grills that used to feed hungry bus passengers in a hurry have been replaced by a fast-food outlet, and the hamburgers cost $2.

Buses still leave and get there on time, and ours pulled into Washington's rush-hour traffic right on schedule. No one is better at fighting city traffic than a professional bus driver, and ours had us rolling south into Virginia in record time.

Trains are communities that come together for the trip, but riding a bus, like riding an airplane, is a solitary affair. You can sit in the club car and make friends on a train, but a 40-seat bus with 15 people on board is a place where you sit alone.

We headed down Interstate 95; first stop, Fredericksburg, Va. It is a one-hour trip, and several of the people on our bus seemed to be daily commuters with briefcases.

Then it was on to Richmond.

The ride was long and endless. The passengers fell silent as the sun went down, leaving us in the dark to watch our reflections in the darkened windows as we passed cars and trucks passed us. It was a time for wide-awake night dreams.

A pretty young girl rode across the aisle. She wore tight jeans, high boots, a skimpy halter top, and from four seats away you could hear the heavy metal music from her radio headset. Others took restless naps. On the back seat, two young soldiers with tattoos and short hair smoked cigarettes.

The bus station in Richmond was a faded memory of what it used to be. Once it was a warm, bustling place with huge murals of downtown scenes painted on the high walls. I had been there before, but now it was like visiting an old friend to whom the years had not been kind. The pay lockers were all empty, and the warm food came from a microwave.

Still on time, we rolled out. We lost some people in Richmond but picked up some construction workers who had smuggled beer on board. That is against the rules, but no one minded. They sat silently and sipped their way to Petersburg.

There were but eight of us left as we headed south from Petersburg on Interstate 85 for the long ride on the night bus to Raleigh.

Memories came back of the cross-country bus trip I took from Wilson, N.C., to El Paso, Texas, in 1962. I thought of the thriving bus stations and the throngs that jammed each one back before everyone could afford to fly. Now we were down to eight people in the darkness, and the bus station in South Hill, Va., is a convenience store off I-85.

Same thing in Henderson. The bus stopped at the Best Bet, and one old woman got on.

The last few miles to Raleigh were sad ones. I had tried to find the romance I truly used to feel on the big buses, but it was gone. They are still running and getting people to places they couldn't get to otherwise — and for that I am grateful — but it wasn't the way it used to be.

The bus seemed old and tired. Or maybe I was.

The night bus to Raleigh pulled in five minutes early. The station in Raleigh is just as modern, clean and safe as the bus station in Washington, but it, too, is a cookie-cutter look-alike.

The two soldiers got off to stretch. They spoke to the girl in tight jeans and asked her where they were. They had been asleep when the driver announced we were in Raleigh.

"I think it's Raleigh," she said. But she didn't seem sure.

My six-hour night bus to Raleigh had become their night bus to Augusta, Ga. They still had nine gritty hours to ride.

I walked home down Blount Street, feeling old.

Let's Solve Some Problems

It is about time.

I've been trying to tell the Popsicle people for years that the two-stick things didn't work.

No matter how carefully I pulled them apart, one side would always break off about half way up. I'd end up with a little nub of a Popsicle in one hand and this humongous, lopsided thing in the other.

Since I tended to do my Popsicle sharing with large, insistent dudes just a few years shy of their first felony, guess which side I got?

Now two-stick Popsicles have gone the way of metal drink cartons. They have entered the realm of boring stories that start, "When I was your age . . . "

Now that the Popsicle problem has been solved, I call on other munchie moguls to clean up their acts as well.

Is it possible in a nation that turns commode water automatically green or blue to produce instant hot chocolate mix that really will dissolve? You can use water so boiling hot that it will remove paint and you can stir it until your arm cramps, but there will be a sludge at the bottom of the cup.

Why doesn't sugar dissolve in iced tea? More and more restaurants are serving unsweetened iced tea — my suspicion is they are trying to attract non-Southern diners — and there is not enough sugar on the average table to properly sweeten iced and unsweetened tea. If you put enough in there to get the top of the tea sweet, the bottom half of the glass tastes like pudding.

Hershey candy bars are fine things — dark, rich and full of good chocolate flavor. But unless you eat them in refrigerated rooms, you are going to wear some chocolate for the rest of the day. They melt so easily that you find yourself licking the gooey remnants off the wrapping paper, and it gets all over your nose.

Barflies will declare a national holiday when they get rid of that red dye they put on vending-machine pistachio nuts. You chow down on a few handfuls of tavern pistachios, and it takes bleach to clean your stained fingertips. Try saying you had to work late when your fingers look like they've been bleeding.

You want to get rich? Find some way to remove cotton candy leavings from around the mouth of a squirming 5-year-old without removing the first layer of skin. A little spit on a mother's pocketbook hanky is not up to the task. Steel wool is effective if a bit drastic.

The paper that is used to make snow cones is hardy stuff, except where it counts. That little portion down at the tip, down where the good stuff sinks, is apparently made of water-soluble tissue paper. It takes awhile to suck down a good snow cone, and the tip is dripping long before you are through with it.

It is has been years since I've had a decent milk shake, the kind made with real milk and real, hand-dipped ice-cream in a metal cup on a whirring Hamilton Beach mixer. No self-respecting cow would admit parentage of the '80s high-tech version served in fast food joints. The ones today are either indigestible gunk or, if they try to do it the old way, they leave huge globs of ice cream hiding in the shake. You tilt one of those things up to your face and you can see that big glop come sliding down to land between your nose and your mouth. But you see it too late to do anything about it.

I want the folks at Coca-Cola, now that they've finally admitted the error of their ways and brought back Real Thing, to go one step further and admit what all of us have known for generations: The Coke in the little glass bottle is better. They can talk until they are thirsty about how all Coke is the the same, but you and I know better, don't we?

Powdered doughnuts that do not leave bearded men looking like they've been snorting cocaine would be nice; and give us a taco shell that does not shatter at first bite.

Kentucky Fried Chicken is good stuff indeed but I would like them to identify the parts of the chicken they are serving. I've been around chickens all my life, both fried and alive, eating it at home and on the road, and I have never seen a chicken with parts like that.

Then maybe we can take care of take-out coffee cup lids that cannot be removed without spilling hot coffee on your hands and pants.

Once all the uncooperative food has been taken care of, we will be able to turn our collective attention to the really nasty things, like public rest room toilet paper rolls that won't and paper towel dispensers that don't.

The Posing of Mary Ellen

As my mama used to say in moments of intense shock and moral outrage, "Well, I never in all my born day . . . ."

I'm with you, Mama.

Did you see Playboy magazine? Did you see those pictures?

Right there, on the slick pages of that magazine, was one of America's idols, a symbol for our youth, the flower of young womanhood, buck nekkid.

Mary Ellen Walton, when your daddy gets hold of you, you won't be able to sit down for a week. Now you march right back into that house this minute, young lady, and get some clothes on. You hear me?

It has almost become a monthly ritual. What usually clothed American woman, willingly or unwillingly, will be displayed au naturel with a staple through her tummy this month?

There was our sad Miss America, Vanessa Williams. Suzanne Somers was angry when Playboy ran her 9-year-old pictures, although she had posed willingly and for pay. But then Ms. Somers realized that the display seemed to help her career, so she did it willingly a few months later.

We had Vicki LaMotta, wife of Jake the former boxer, showing the world what it knew already, that 50-year-old women can be gorgeous. Roxanne Pulitzer posed nude with the legendary trumpet. Brooke Shields did it as a pre-teen, and one, having seen her clothed and unclothed as an almost-adult, is permitted to wonder why. I was, at worst, amused by these antics. I was never shocked.

And then there was Madonna. It seems that the only magazine that did not have nude pictures of this month's Hottest Performer of the Decade was the Progressive Farmer. She was everywhere. Penthouse first announced that it had some pictures of Madonna naked. Playboy said it did, too, nyah-nyah. Just last week, hundreds, yes hundreds, of newspapers around the world ran 6-year-old pictures of the slightly pudgy, one-name wonder in the nude.

But you kind of expect that sort of thing from Madonna. Let's face it; she sings "Like a Virgin," but she sure doesn't look or act like one. Her image is that of a yard-sale trollop, and that's fine and funny and somehow charming and engaging.

Her image in the magazines, however, is slob. There is nothing sexy about her at all. She looks like a bored young woman who was hired to take her clothes off, and as soon as the shutter snapped, she picked up her paycheck and went home and defrosted the fridge.

I was around in the hippie-dippie 1960s, and I got used to women who didn't shave their legs or their underarms. They looked just fine. Madonna Louise Ciccone, however, is not one of them. Had she not become a star, those pictures never would have been printed anywhere but in the Razor Blade Digest, and then only as the girl they'd most like to get close to. The woman is fuzzy all over.

But no one seemed to notice when Mary Ellen Walton, the little girl who wanted to be a nurse and marry a doctor and take care of sick people on Walton's Mountain, Va., dressed up in her black Halloween Harlot outfit and put on her lipstick for the previous month's Playboy. She did not get that outfit at Ike Godsey's store, I can tell you that.

Yes, she was wearing lipstick. Our little Mary Ellen. A painted lady. I was shocked, too.

Then our little Mary Ellen went on television's "Hour Magazine" with the shopworn excuse that she didn't know the pictures were going to come out looking like that.

Excuse me, Mary Ellen, but when you put on black stockings and a black garter belt and black rhinestone shoes and dangly earbobs and black gloves up to your elbows with a purple ring on the outside of the glove and that's all you're wearing, sweetheart, you are not posing for passport pictures no matter what those fast-talking city slickers tell you.

Of course, she doesn't answer to Mary Ellen anymore. She calls herself Judy Norton-Taylor these days.

All I can say is, I'd change my name, too, after such shocking behavior.

Wearing a ring on the outside of her glove? Well, I never in all my born days.

Fruitcake Disposal Guide

It is January and time to ponder the question: What to do with the fruitcake?

The tree and the first layer of needles embedded in the carpet are gone, but the fruitcake remains like the last guest who will not leave.

The toys are broken, but the fruitcake is whole. One wool sweater has been washed in hot water and has shrunk even smaller than the bank account, but the fruitcake seems to be getting bigger and bigger. The refrigerator shelf is beginning to buckle. Something must be done.

I have some suggestions for holiday fruitcakes.

Put the fruitcake in the trunk of your car. The added weight will give better traction when the roads get icy, and you can use it to chock your wheels when you park your car on hills. In case of a flat tire, put it underneath the jack to keep it from sinking into the soft ground.

Go around the neighborhood and collect all the fruitcakes from your neighbors. In addition to making friends for life, you can use them for neighborhood improvement projects. Line a group of them up across the street to make an instant speed bump that lasts through the ages. Please do not stack them more than one high or they will rip out the underside of a car.

Stack a lot of them up, paint them red like a fire hydrant and place the resulting sculpture where there are a lot of city dogs.

Schools are often short of athletic equipment; your leftover fruitcakes can help. They make excellent shot puts but make sure the kids are big enough to handle such serious weight. The Little League baseball team can use them as bases. Stacked high enough, they make great blocking dummies — but only when the team is in full pads and helmets.

Boaters are in luck. Take the fruit cake from the kitchen — remember to bend at the knees when lifting it or, better yet, have help — and haul it out to the garage. Let it sit there until summer and use it as an anchor on those boating excursions. A heavy-duty drill equipped with a masonry bit, and some patience, will eventually allow you to make a hole large enough to tie a chain through. Remember not to overload the boat when carrying the fruitcake anchor. It will take the place of at least one adult.

Those who own seagoing craft can load up as many fruitcakes as is safe and haul them offshore to their favorite fishing spot and dump them to create an artificial reef. Make sure you notify the Coast Guard so they can mark their charts. You would not want a steel-hulled warship crushing its hull on your fruitcake reef.

One word of warning to apartment dwellers: Never store your fruitcake on the second floor. Local building codes do not permit such stress on floor joists. Water beds are fine, however.

A fruitcake that is too hard and heavy to move can still be used constructively. Rent or borrow a chain saw (make sure the chain is a new one) and slice the fruitcake. Remember to wear goggles. Flying bits of citron can do permanent damage.

The resulting slices have many uses. One favorite for local gun fanciers is to use them as targets for skeet shooting. The best part is that you can reuse the targets no matter how many times they have been hit by shotgun pellets. Make sure the range is clear before throwing the slices into the air. You wouldn't want someone to get hurt when they fall to the ground.

The slices also are good for repairing flagstone patios. Most people will never notice that the fruitcake slices are harder than the surrounding stones. Wear steel-toed boots when doing this work. Safety first.

Just for the heck of it, box up your fruitcake and mail it to Ayatollah Khomeini in Iran. The postage will be steep, but the great personal satisfaction will be worth it.

There are some things you should not do with a fruitcake.

Do not give into temptation and use it as a doorstop. A visitor may stub a toe on it. You might check whether that is covered by your homeowner's policy, but most do not cover accidents caused by dangerous items kept in the home.

Under no circumstances should you throw the fruitcake into the yard assuming that it will decay. It will be there, intact, when the summer comes and could seriously damage your lawn mower blade.

A Memory-Filled Bottle

Most people would look at the beer bottle on top of my file cabinet in my study and say, "Look, a useless old beer bottle with penicillin growing in the bottom of it."

What do they know about memories?

Moving is the pits. It makes you look at and touch everything you own and throw a lot of it away. You're getting married, old boy, and it is time to grow up.

I've been packing for the past several days as I get ready for my move from the old home in downtown Raleigh to the house in North Raleigh. (Homes are what you move from and houses are what you move to.) The work isn't all that tough since I had furnished my home in what might best be called Minimalist Spartan. Less is better and a whole lot cheaper. I live alone, and how many chairs can I possibly sit in at one time?

But while I don't have a lot of furniture, I sure have a lot of memories. Like the beer bottle.

It is an ordinary Heineken bottle. My friend Dale Gibson and I were coming back from a football game in Chapel Hill in the fall of 1981. Carolina had lost 10-8 to Clemson, one of only two losses that great year, and we stopped at a convenience store and picked up a six-pack of "Greenies" to soothe our raw throats. Dale and I used to yell a lot at Carolina games, back when there was a lot to yell about.

We drank all but one of that six-pack, and as I headed to the apartment I was living in then, I took the last beer with me. It was a disappointing loss and I was mulling it over when, out of the blue, I said to myself that I was going to keep that last beer, unopened, until Carolina won a national championship in either football or basketball. I put the beer in the refrigerator and left it there.

There were a lot of parties that winter at my place, and a lot of beer was brought in and drunk by me and visitors as we gathered to watch the Heels play basketball. But not the little bottle of Heineken. I'd hide it behind the mayo when friends were coming over, just so it wouldn't be opened by mistake or by a thirsty fan. But after they left, I'd put it back on the shelf. Often it was alone in the fridge. I'd see it and remember my pledge.

It came to be the night of March 29, 1982. We gathered at my place to watch the Heels take on Georgetown for the national championship. Things got off to a tough start with the Hoyas leading for most of the first half. But the Heels hung tough, and the little bottle of Heineken was sitting way back in the fridge. It had been chilling for five months.

The lead changed hands 13 times in the second half in one of the greatest basketball games ever played anywhere. The Hoyas had a one-point lead with 32 seconds to go in the game. The Heels brought the ball down court as the clock ticked away. With 17 seconds to go, the ball went to freshman Michael Jordan on the left side, and he jumped high in the Louisiana Superdome and swished one from 18 feet out.

We went nuts. We were still screaming as the Hoyas' Fred Brown brought the ball back up court with plenty of time left, only to pass it straight into the hands of rock-steady James Worthy of Carolina, and it was all over. The roar in my apartment was deafening — and my neighbor was banging on the wall for us to shut up — as I went into the kitchen and got that bottle of beer.

I popped the top, said a quiet thank you to Dean Smith, and chugged that long-chilled beer. I still remember how good it tasted. Then I went back into the madness in my living room and poured the remains on Dale Gibson's balding dome.

After it was all over, I sat that empty bottle on top of my file cabinet, and it has been there since. I'd see it and remember that night.

I held it again the other day while I was packing and remembered the night I drank it. There was no reason to take it to the new house. It would look tacky, wouldn't it, to have an empty beer bottle sitting in a nice house? Old beer bottles are for college boys and bachelor pads, not suburban ranch houses with neat lawns and married folks.

So I tossed the little Heineken bottle into a trash box, in with the old ticket stubs from Willie Nelson concerts, my member

ship card to Music City, some brochures from my trip to Bike
Week in Daytona Beach, Fla., and a map of the London subway
system. Just a box of old memories from a life that was forever
changed that Saturday when I pledged my love and future to
Gail Knowlton.

I hope she understood when I pulled that little beer bottle out of
the trash and took it with me to our new house.

You Were Young Once, Too

Amy Carol Joyner stood in the well of the old House Chamber
in the historic North Carolina State Capitol and faced the people
who had come to listen to her speak.

Her voice was strong and self-assured as she began to talk
about the Constitution of the United States. If she was nervous, it
did not show. If she had any doubts about her facts, she covered
them well. If there was any fear that she would not win the
regional competition of the American Legion National High
School Oratorical Contest, you could not tell it.

No one in the audience bore her anything but good wishes, but
my job, and the job of the other judges, was to be critical, to look
for mistakes, to find a flaw in her argument or her delivery.

We found few things to criticize, and when the morning was
over, Amy, 18 and a senior from Lee County Senior High School,
had won the four-state regional competition. She had bested
speakers from Virginia, West Virginia and Tennessee and was
on her way to Little Rock, Ark., for the sectional competition.

I must confess that my mind drifted sometimes while Amy and
the three other young women were speaking (all four of the state
winners were female). I kept thinking about kids.

Sometimes it is hard not to have a nagging feeling that we
don't like our kids very much. We say some awful things about
them.

Maybe the old complaint is true. Maybe the good kids don't
attract much attention. Recently, the nation has been shocked
and saddened by the suicides of four teenagers in New Jersey.
Immediately the cry goes up: What is wrong with our kids?

There are stories about teenage murderers. Drug use among
teenagers is said to be epidemic. Kids are more sexually active
but less informed about birth control. Teenage parents are

trying to raise children while they are little more than children themselves.

They wear funny clothes and do odd things to their hair. They listen to awful music and seem to run in raging packs. They have no respect for their elders and ignore the wisdom we have to offer. What is wrong with our kids?

Not much, I think.

For every kid using crack in a high school parking lot, there are dozens like Amy, who spent weeks researching her 10-minute speech on the Constitution. For every young couple making babies after school, there are hundreds making good grades and learning more by the time they finish high school than earlier generations learned in college.

I watched the kids in a recent charity walkathon in Raleigh, trudging through rotten weather to help other people. The math and science high school in Durham is jammed with the best and the brightest of our state. Go into any fast-food restaurant and you'll see teenagers working as hard as their elders ever worked.

I go into schools from time to time, and every time, I am besieged with questions from bright-eyed kids who want to know. For every dullard who sits in the back of the classroom and sleeps, there are dozens who want to learn, and they ask tough questions.

Kids don't make or sell the music and print the magazines and produce the rock videos some adults are so sure are harming them. Adults do that; they determine what kids will see on television or at the movies. I have seen the film "Platoon" twice and on each occasion there were teenagers in the audience who watched closely and wanted to understand. I watched them leave the theaters with real concern on their faces.

We adults seem to forget that we were ever young. We never slipped out to the parking lot at a high school basketball game and drank beer, did we? We didn't listen to music that our parents thought was awful, did we? We didn't wear our hair in ducktails and wear leather jackets with turned-up collars, did we? We didn't talk back to parents, did we? We were perfect, weren't we?

What's wrong with the kids today?

Nothing. They're just kids in the 1980s. They are no better or worse than we were and they have just as much chance of success as we did. It might be good to remember that not all of our generation, or any other generation, did so well either.

There are losers out there, teenagers and adults, who have never succeeded in life and never will. Perhaps we spend too much time worrying about the few culls and too little time patting the good ones on the back.

Amy Joyner is one of the good ones, and she is not alone.

Lots of Food for Thought

I was sitting there bleary-eyed at dawn, drinking coffee and pondering the eternally important question raised by my morning newspaper: Where does The Phantom get those funky skin-tight clothes he wears?

A hunger pang gnawed through my literary concentration, so I grabbed a bagel, toasted it and commenced to smear it generously with cream cheese and strawberry jam.

Then it hit me: Of all the great food inventions lauded by mankind in recent years, few can compare with spreadable cream cheese. It is great stuff, a boon to anyone who has ever tried to spread cold cream cheese on anything.

I looked around me. I was surrounded by great strides in modern food technology, and not a one of them has ever made the cover of Time magazine.

There is an easy way to tell whether something is truly a great invention. If you take one look at it, understand immediately how it works and then say to yourself, "Why didn't somebody think of that before?" Then you've got a truly great invention.

Like ketchup in a squeeze bottle. Restaurants have been using those red plastic ketchup bottles for years, but we at home were stuck with glass bottles that held our ketchup inside more securely than a new mama holds a baby in her arms. One ketchup company tried to promote its ketchup as the slowest — something I found hard to get excited about — but that went the way of the Edsel when the squeeze bottle hit the shelf. No more knives down the neck of the bottle, no more looking at that black stuff around the top and wondering if it will kill you, no more banging on the bottom of the bottle that resulted in big glops of out-of-control ketchup.

I knew someone one day would come up with a good use for the microwave oven, and they have: microwave popcorn. Called "nuclear popcorn" by many, we popcorn fans have taken to the microwave stuff with a passion. You actually can pop a good-size batch of really great popcorn between television shows. You give it four minutes or so, and it comes out hot, tender and with darned few old maids. No oil to measure, no greasy popper to clean; just pop it in, take it out and you're through in time for Max Headroom.

Popcorn has long been a problem for food technologists and spawned one of the really bad inventions of modern kitchens: the hot air popper. It makes popcorn just fine, but salt won't stick to it, and what good is popcorn without salt?

For most of us, the food processor is nothing but a high-tech version of the good old late-night-TV Vegamatic. It is an expensive thing with a zillion parts that will chop an onion in a nanosecond but takes hours to disassemble, clean and put back together. Compare it with the always-on-duty ice maker. There is a special place in heaven for the inventor of the ice maker. Families have been held together who once would have shattered over the eternal problem of "Who forgot to fill up the ice trays?" There is always ice, and anyone who grew up in the days of iceboxes can applaud that.

I have found a new treasure in recent months that I love a lot: little jars of chopped garlic. Garlic, like niacin, riboflavin and iron, is one of the essential ingredients in most foods. A dish without garlic is hardly worth eating, but mincing several cloves of garlic is a boring, messy job. You never get it small enough, and somebody always bites down in the hunk you got tired of chopping and threw in whole. No more. Open the jar, use a half-teaspoon for each clove and keep on cooking. Great stuff, and it comes in two sizes, chopped and minced. I like to keep both on hand.

Peach schnapps. This stuff is incredible. Peach lovers have long complained that canned peaches don't taste even vaguely like fresh peaches, but an ounce of peach schnapps in a glass of orange juice tastes exactly like a nectar of tree-ripened fresh peaches. A consumer warning, however: The resulting drink is called a Fuzzy Navel and goes down real, real easy. Be careful.

But the best kitchen invention of recent years, the one thing you'll find in any modern American home, the most efficient, cheap, durable helpmate of all is the refrigerator magnet. What a great idea! No more hunting for the tape to stick Junior's drawing on the fridge. No more littering the top of the fridge with stuff you need to keep. Just stick it on and forget it.

Now why didn't I think of that?

A Rock-Solid Generation

Let's call them Joe and Betty, two rock-solid, all-American names to represent a rock-solid, all-American generation.

You probably know them by other names. If you are family folks in your 40s, you call them Mom and Dad. If you're a kid, they're your grandparents.

Joe and Betty are retired now. If they were lucky, they can take it easy, travel a little, work in the yard, have some time for civic clubs and visit the kids. If they were not lucky, they're living hand-to-mouth on Social Security checks and worried about the rising cost of utilities, food and medical care.

It is human nature to think that your generation is the only one that matters, that you have done more, been more, seen more, worked harder and know more than anyone else. That could be, but I'd like to say a word today for Joe and Betty and the folks like them. There really is something special about them.

They're 68 now. There were born in 1919, and they were Baby Boomers, too. Their dads came home from The Great War, which is what they called it until they had another one and had to give that first one a number rather than a name, and they and their wives began having babies. That always happens after wars. Seeing death makes humans want to create life.

Joe and Betty's childhood was in the 1920s. They lived on a farm or in a small town, and almost no one had a car. A few folks had radios, but movies were rare entertainments and for city folks. Doctors still made house calls, and everybody worked hard. It was against the law to drink, and everyone knew how to handle a mule.

They were 10 years old when the bottom fell out of their world, and that is a tender age to face something as serious as the Great Depression. There was massive unemployment, no money, no luxuries. People went without food, clothes and decent houses year after year. Joe and Betty really did walk to school carrying their cold biscuits and sweet potato lunches in a lard bucket. They grew to maturity with absolutely no promise of a better life. It didn't seem that it would ever end. There were no colleges or careers waiting for them. No one asked them what they wanted to be when they grew up because there were so few choices. No rainbows decorated that dark decade. There were real doubts that America and democracy could survive.

It was 1936. They were 17 and out of school and out of work. Joe went off to join the Civilian Conservation Corps because it meant honest work, three squares and a cot. Betty stayed at home.

Things were better four years later when they were 21. There was a job in the shipyard for Joe, so they got married. And then there was another war. Joe picked up a gun and went off to fight, and Betty got a job in a defense plant. They were apart for four years, and a lot of people died.

Then they thought they had it made. The war was over, Joe was home, Betty quit her job, they started having babies, and they bought the first house they ever owned. They still might be living in it today. It's too small and the neighborhood is not what it used to be, but it's home and they don't want to leave. There are too many memories there.

The 1950s were wonderful. They worked hard and raised their kids and prospered. Their life was simple but pleasant. It seemed that it would never end.

Then came the '60s, and everything they believed in was turned upside down. A president was assassinated. Men with guns shattered the nation's peaceful slumber. Cities were engulfed in riots. Those kids they had worked so hard to raise turned into something called hippies. It wasn't so much the long hair and the weird music. It was more than that. It was the rejection of the values Joe and Betty had believed in and lived by for so long, the values that had gotten them through the hard times.

Don't trust anyone over 30, the kids said, and that included Joe and Betty. And that hurt because they were good, honest people worthy of being trusted.

Then they lost a son in Vietnam. He died in a war that everyone said was wrong, but although it might have been wrong, Joe Junior was still dead. And that hurt, too.

But they always could believe in their president, couldn't they? Franklin Delano Roosevelt had pulled them through the Depression and a world war, and they believed the man in the White House. But then it was 1974, and the president was a crook and liar and he left in disgrace. That hurt, too.

But they're over that hurt now. Now their kids are the parents. And their children are dyeing their hair orange and shaving half of it off and listening to weird music and rejecting everything their parents stand for. They are driving their parents crazy. On it goes.

Joe and Betty can be forgiven if they smile now at what they see around them. They've earned the right.

Is It Another Joke?

When Ann Landers asked her now-famous question about whether you prefer cuddling to other forms of late-night entertainment, you jumped at the opportunity to pull another of your gags, didn't you?

I laughed so hard my socks fell down when she wrote that 72 percent of you said yeah, hold my hand but nothing else.

I am amazed at your ability to make men dance to your tune like a two-pound trout on a fly rod. You set us up and then when we try to go along with the joke, you jerk us in another direction.

As a twice-married man, it has been my distinct pleasure to make the acquaintance of a number of your delightful gender, and I'll say one thing for you: It has never been boring.

Remember your pedestal? You used to love it up there, prim, proper and pristine while at your feet men groveled, babbled and killed for a smile. How you must have laughed at us while we carried your books and wrote your name on sidewalks and beat on each other to win your favors.

You got bored in the '60s, so you got Mary Quant to invent miniskirts and go-go boots and you played tarts while the boys were still playing hearts.

It took a while, but we got the joke and joined in. We, as you must have expected, drooled and steam came out of our ears and we whistled when you sashayed by with your miniskirt flouncing. It was great, but then you got bored.

"Quit treating us like sex objects," you said, and burned your bras. We poor men were baffled by that seeming contradiction, but we went along.

Gosh, you were funny.

Just when our senses were piqued by your fashions and unfashions, you said, "Stop acting like John Wayne and start acting like Alan Alda."

OK, we bit. If I remember M*A*S*H correctly, Alan Alda was a hard-drinking wise guy who chased everything in a nurse's uniform, so we took you at your word and went at you like a pack of hungry dogs.

No, you said, not like that. Be sensitive. Be sharing. Be gentle.

Yes, ma'am. Pass the quiche and let me tell you my troubles.

That was a good one. Right when we were at our sensitive best, even adding your name and a hyphen to ours when we got married, along came John Travolta with his three-piece white suit with no tie.

How you must have giggled when we showed up at the disco with fake hair plastered on our exposed chests just because we thought that's what you wanted. Then Travolta made "Urban Cowboy" and we bought fancy hats and cowboy boots and learned to two-step. Didn't we look funny, though?

The sexual revolution was in full swing and you were the drill sergeants. You divorced us and we divorced you, and the singles bars were jammed six nights a week. You called us on the phone and you asked us out.

We said, hey, what a deal, here we have liberated women who pay their own way and ask us for dates and Saturday night is more fun than ever.

You probably saw we were enjoying that too much so you did it again. You must have figured out how expensive it was to pay the tab. This time you decided family, home and, most of all, babies, were what you wanted. The early '80s baby boom exploded, and we learned to change diapers and do something called "parenting."

Well, OK, it wasn't as much fun as some of your jokes but you were the only game in town.

You had about convinced us not to treat you as sex objects anymore when, lo and behold, you start treating us as sex objects. Calendars featuring nude males were everywhere. One from last Christmas was memorable. It was called "Buns" and had nothing to do with croissants.

OK, we thought, now we're sex objects, so let's go for it, guys. Sign up for Nautilus work at the spa and get those deltoids in shape. Tighten up the backside. Be a hunk.

And now you tell us that yes, we're supposed to be a hunk, but all you want hunks to do is cuddle. Frankly, that is not what we thought being a hunk meant.

Well, you've had your latest little joke. Now will you please let Ann Landers in on it?

● ● ●

The mail response to those observations was certainly interesting. I don't know when I have so enjoyed being called ugly things.

I was wrong. I admit it. I unfairly lumped all women into one group and I should apologize. So I apologize and set the record straight: All women do not have a sense of humor. Most do, and they got the joke and thought the whole idea was funny. My guess is that they are not part of the now-famous 72 percent.

"Poor Baby, did ums get ums male ego bruised?" one woman from Raleigh poetically snarled. "Snide, contumely and vituperous (Webster helped me, I confess) is how I found your column, not to mention humorless."

"The column was a cheap shot from beginning to end," said another.

Other readers were prompted to share their thoughts about relationships between men and women.

Karen Blow of Raleigh writes, "Poor Dennis Rogers. I mean that. Sincerely I do. But, and correct me if I am wrong, I think that what you are saying is that you (meaning men) are simply confused as to what women want.

"Let me tell you something: Women are just as confused as men.

"We were brought up to believe that if you were a good wife and mommy, you would be taken care of. Next thing we know, the men are divorcing us left and right. We're thrown out into the real world to compete in the free enterprise system.

"If we look like a housewife, we're considered boring. If we look like the 'total woman,' we're not taken seriously. If we're the dependent kind, a man wants us to be strong. If we're strong, a man's ego gets bruised because we don't need him.

"We're damned if we do and damned if we don't. We have to wear 20 hats and be able to change them at a moment's notice. We have to be mommy, daddy, career woman, femme fatale."

Cleo Parker Austin of Four Oaks writes: "Your column was hilarious. I hadn't realized that men regarded women as being so fickle as you portrayed us to be. We must be doing something right, because the piper keeps dancing to our tune.

"I am delighted to know that my species is never boring. We might make your manhood struggle, but hopefully you'll have no regrets when you retire to your recliner to reflect on what you call the long line of women's jokes. What in the world would men do without us?"

This comes from a Raleigh woman who asked that her name not be used: "Right on! Your article really hits pay dirt.

"I'm a woman, and I've been a party to much of the double messages also. Women are trying to find themselves, their own identity and their independence. Yet a great many of them still hang onto the old ideas of being taken care of, cuddled and physical appearances determining their value.

"Too many women are trying to play both games, one minute

trying to be the professional and the next flouncing their physical attributes to gain favor. It is no wonder the males are turned off, for they probably never know what game is being played at the time."

All joking aside, I've learned something from what started out as gentle ribbing. We've all, men and women, still got a long way to go before we can openly approach each other without anger, suspicion and hostility. Every man who makes a joke about women is not a male chauvinist pig. Every woman who demands to be treated as an equal is not trying to emasculate men.

I keep thinking about what Karen Blow wrote: "Admit it, we are all victims. We all want to be loved. We all want to be taken seriously. Maybe when we stop being so defensive with each other, stop trying to compete, stop trying to be all things to all people, maybe then both sexes will come to the same conclusion: Nobody's perfect, and we all basically want the same things."

Smuggler's Blues

We were standing beneath the palm trees that line the cove near Ocho Rios, Jamaica, when the secret deal went down on that pretty afternoon. It was hot, but the trade winds were blowing in off the Spanish Main and were keeping things comfortable.

There was the heartbeat rhythm of reggae music and the sweet scent of bougainvillea in the air as the blood-warm, too-blue-to-believe waters of the Caribbean whispered ashore a few feet away. The white sand was fine beneath my bare feet.

He was a tall, black man dressed all in white. He had the physique of an exclamation mark and he had mirrored sunglasses that kept the bright Caribbean sun away from his eyes. I could see nothing but myself when I looked into his thin face.

I sidled up to him cautiously, trying not to be nervous as I looked around to see whether we were being watched. Things looked peaceful, but you never know. Women in bikinis were baking in the sun and sailboats played on the water. It was time to do the deal. This was the way he'd said it had to be done.

"You got to give me some squeeze, mon," he'd said in his lilting island accent when I'd asked him earlier about the good stuff. I wasn't exactly sure what that meant, but I had a good idea. I had to be real cool.

I folded two Jamaican $10 bills into the palm of my right hand and flashed them so he could see I had more than skin and best wishes to offer when I reached out to shake his hand.

His face broke into a grin as he took my hand and gave it a squeeze. I never felt the two crisp bills go from my hand to his.

"No problem, mon," he said, putting his hand in his pocket and making it look natural. "I take care of you and you take care of me, mon."

Then he gave me the stuff I wanted. I wrapped it in my beach towel and headed for my room to stash it.

The reggae music kept playing and the Red Stripe beer kept flowing at the pool bar as I gave my beautiful partner a little nod that only she could see. She smiled.

We had scored some "jerk." Now we had to get it back into the United States.

Atlanta, Ga., two days later: It was a cold, wet, dismal day when the Air Jamaica jet landed. We collected our baggage and headed for the U.S. Customs desk. The customs inspectors were wearing guns and badges.

I picked the shortest line. There was a woman at the desk. I handed her our passports, but she didn't look at them.

"What did you buy in Jamaica?" she asked. Could she have known? Was it all a setup?

"Just some rum, some tablecloths and some cheap souvenirs," my beautiful partner told her. I kept quiet.

Then the inspector cleared us and we'd made it. We were home free with "jerk" packed in the dirty clothes in the luggage.

Every word of this account is true. It isn't very pretty what a man will do when he has found the best barbecue sauce in the world and has to have some for his very own.

They call the sauce "jerk" in Jamaica, and two weeks ago, on our honeymoon, my bride and I tasted it for the first time. There was no discussion; we had to have some to bring home. It is a thick, spicy, pungent, almost black sauce heavenly laden with hot peppers and Jamaican "Pickapeppa" sauce. It will clear your sinuses and make your taste buds dance. It is the taste of Jamaica.

You marinate chicken or pork (jerk chicken is wonderful and jerk pork is even better) in a little bit of the stuff for 24 hours and then you either bake the meat or cook it on a grill. We ate it for lunch six of the seven days we were there and never got enough of it.

I approached the chef presiding over the grill on the beach early in the week to tell him how wonderful his jerk chicken and pork were and to inquire about buying some sauce. Our hotel had a rule against the staff taking money from guests, but hey, this was Jamaica. He hinted that for a quiet $20 Jamaican on the side (less than $4 U.S.) he could fix me up. No problem. They sell a perfectly legal version in gift shops but I wanted the homemade, authentic kind.

My bride even cadged the recipe from him so when our bottle is empty we can try to make it on our own.

Americans have gone through the fad foods of sushi and Cajun blackened fish in recent years. Jerk, I predict, will be the next food to tickle our taste buds. It already is at our house. And to show you what a nice guy I am, I will pass along the recipe after we've had a chance to mix up a test batch.

But it won't be as much fun as we had buying it on that beautiful Jamaican beach.

Dreams Go Up in Smoke

You may have heard that CBS would be broadcasting its morning news/talk show from Raleigh.

You may have heard also, especially if you have been within earshot of me for the past month, that I was going to be on that very same television show, espousing the glories of Eastern North Carolina barbecue to a waiting America.

Well, like my old daddy used to say, you can't always believe what you hear.

I was canceled. Shown the door. Given the boot. Canned. I feel like McLean Stevenson.

This was going to be my big shot at stardom. Here I'd waited 45 years to be on national television and show the world what a clever, erudite, charming and, dare I say it, devilishly handsome and some would say quite sexy fellow I really am. I've tried to do it in print for 20 years, but that little black-and-white mug shot they run with this column doesn't show my cute blue eyes at their best. No, it would take television to do it. Someday, I figured, with the right breaks, I'd be bigger than Jim Bakker and Pee Wee Herman combined.

This was it, the Big Break. I was going to be sitting there on national television with none other than the hottest of the hot babes of morning television, Kathleen Sullivan. It never occurred to me for an instant that I might get stuck with the bald-headed guy who is her co-host. No, it would be me and Kathleen and I'd charm her mascara off.

We know what would happen then, don't we? In three, maybe four, weeks I'd have a show of my own and so much money that I'd hire the bald-headed guy just to count it. Hot and cold running lackeys would be at my beck and call. Network VP's would chew their Guccis to keep me happy . . . and I'd be a darned hard man to please.

Let's face it, CBS is the third-place network and it needs all the help it can get. I would do for CBS what Hill Street Blues did for NBC.

But no. Not for me, thank you.

I still can't believe they did this to me. A CBS producer named Emily Lazar called me six weeks ago and practically begged me to be on television talking about the joys of eating the Holy Grub. I modestly agreed and then proceeded to get a serious case of the Big Head. I managed to work the news into every conversation I had for a month.

"Sure, Jesse Jackson poses a very sensitive problem for the Democrats, but when I'm on national TV next month . . . ." "Sure, I'll take out the garbage, but I can't do it next Monday morning, you know, because I'll be on national television. . . ."

People got real tired of hearing that, but I didn't care. I was shameless. I wrote a column that was to slyly hype my appearance, although I was very coy about it and tried not to make it sound like hype. But it was.

I even got nervous for several days. I had a lot of work to do and all I could think about was what I ought to wear on TV. I had it narrowed down to jeans, cowboy boots and a Harley-Davidson T-shirt or The One Suit I Own. I had my VCR all ready to tape it in case anyone missed it.

But then came the call right after lunch. It was from a woman named Mary Murphy and she said, "I'm sorry, but we've canceled the barbecue segment." And then she gave some lame line like, "I hope we can do it again some day."

Sure you do, Ms. Murphy. And pigs fly.

I'm just crushed. Not only have I been canceled, but this allegedly professional television network thinks it can come down here and do two hours about North Carolina and not mention Tar Heel barbecue, much less mention me.

No wonder CBS is in third place. If it keeps this up, it'll come in just behind one of those home shopping networks in the next ratings.

But no, the TV lights will come up on time right at 7 a.m. Kathleen will be beautiful, the other guy will be bald and I'll be at home, sitting in my underwear, unshaven, drinking coffee and watching the Today Show on NBC.

I won't be on there, either, but at least it didn't break my heart.

Raleigh's Finest to Rescue

I feel sorry for folks who live in neat little subdivisions in the peaceful suburbs. What do they do for excitement?

Those of us who live in old houses in the middle of Raleigh never lack for entertainment and squirts of adrenaline to pep up boring nights.

Take one recent ordinary Wednesday night. A friend and I had been to the movies, and we had gotten back to my house in the city around 11 p.m.

I was babbling about something or other when my friend shushed me.

"Did you hear something," she said.

Then we both heard it. Something was coughing, and the sound was coming through a heating duct. The cougher was in my basement.

"My God, the Thing that Lives in My Basement has a cold," I thought before I came to my senses and realized that my basement was not really haunted. Or at least I didn't think it was.

Then it coughed again, and I knew we had us a little problem.

I didn't want to panic, so I decided that I had to find out if indeed I did have someone in my basement or perhaps it was some wino in the yard outside the window. But I knew I was not going out in the dark armed with nothing more than good intentions and liberal ideology. I looked around for an M-16, but I'd left it overseas almost 20 years ago. Clearly an oversight on my part.

So I grabbed my trusty K-Bar knife (ask a veteran what that is) and thus armed, I creeped around the side of my house with a sense of deja vu you wouldn't believe. I tried hard to remember all the things I had learned in knife-fighting class in the Army, but then I remembered I was on KP the day they taught that class.

Halfway along the dark side of my house, it coughed again. Yep, something was in my basement.

I did the wise thing and retreated to the phone. God bless 911, because if I'd had one more digit to dial, my nervous fingers might not have found it. That simple call set in motion a most impressive display of the Raleigh Police Department on the job.

With heart in throat, I told the dispatcher who answered on the first ring that someone was in my basement. He told me to stay on the phone, and I heard him send police cars.

He kept me talking to him on the phone, I suspect, because that would keep me away from whoever was in my basement, and thereby safe, and it would have me out of the way when the police officers arrived. Officers responding to that kind of call do not want to have to figure out who are the good guys and who are the bad guys in the dark.

In less than three minutes, a police car silently came to a stop in front of my house. "Hill Street Blues" had come to life.

By the time I had hung up and gotten to the door, three cars had arrived and I had not heard them. Three no-nonsense officers, who barely make enough money to live on, were prowling in the dark around my house to find God knows what waiting for them.

It didn't take them long to solve the Mystery of the Coughing Basement.

A neighborhood wino had unlocked an outside basement access door and crawled inside to spend the night. He came out willingly, if a bit drunkenly, to find himself staring into a lot of flashlights.

They frisked him and reassured me that he was harmless. Then they asked me what I wanted them to do with him. Let him slide, I said, but let him know if he does it again, he's going to jail.

They told me to tell him that, with three of them as witnesses, so it would be official. I did, and the apologetic wino tottered off down the street.

I felt a little sorry for him when I went into my basement. He was set for the night. He'd found an old drape to wrap around him. He had left behind a full bottle of Thunderbird wine and, on the way out, had dropped two new packs of cigarettes. My night had been exciting, but his was a total bust.

I've got to hand it to those officers. They were there quickly, handled the wino professionally but with compassion and not once did they make me feel foolish for wasting their time on some derelict.

Thanks, officers.

Fathers Love Their Day

Mothers are used to constant adulation from their young. Kids are always coming home from school with something they made for Mom, such as a hot mat made from ice cream sticks or a picture painted on a paper plate. Big, burly football players always look at the sideline cameras and say "Hi, Mom" right after they've torn the head off some opposing player. Dedicating their mayhem to Mom is their way of telling Mom how much she means to them.

Dads don't get that sort of continuing flow of gratitude. For us, it gets saved up until the middle of June. And when it comes, we are reduced to puddles of grinning.

We don't have to pretend to have all the answers on Father's Day. We don't have to be the strong, silent types. We don't have to pretend to have an inexhaustible wallet. We can just be silly old Dad.

Most dads love Father's Day. It ranks right up there in our hearts with opening day of the ACC basketball tournament. We scan the newspaper ads for the preceding week, secretly wondering which of the advertised goodies we'll get this year. I never get any of them, but I am never disappointed. I always get something much better. This year was no exception.

Each Father's Day, a lot of us dads are reminded that we are the lucky ones. We did our small part to help rear some very nice people. I would like my daughters even if I had not been their father.

I realize that I had very little to do with the successful women my little girls have turned out to be. They surely were not reared in the traditional way. They had to move around a lot when they were young, and we didn't have much money. For most of their childhood, Dad was a soldier, a college student and a traveling journalist. But they made it anyway. They packed up their toys when the time came, sniffled in the back seat as we drove away and kept on trying to understand. But they made it with strong spirits and good hearts intact.

Little girls fixing a Father's Day breakfast for Dad is an old and honored way to begin Father's Day. We've done it a lot at our house, and like most dads, I get all blubbery and adore every one of them.

But things have changed. When we dads and daughters were younger, breakfast used to be burned, or runny, eggs; bacon, either burned or limp; and toast, usually cold. But we'd sit there grinning and eating. Bad food never tasted better.

One day when we weren't looking, they grew up. And the news hit me square in the face this year.

Denise came home from Winston-Salem, where she is a married woman with a house and a job. We went out to dinner and a movie Saturday night. We had a little time to wait before the movie, so I suggested that we kill 30 minutes in a bar near the theater. I was floating on a sea of fatherlike nostalgia, and then my little girl ordered bourbon, and the bartender didn't even ask her for an ID card.

It hit me: My little girl is a 24-year-old married woman. How in the world did that happen?

It came to be Sunday morning. Melanie arrived early from her apartment across town with a bag of food and big plans for breakfast. This was not to be a morning of runny eggs and burned bacon.

In almost less time than it takes to tell it, she whipped up my most favorite breakfast in the world: eggs Benedict, the best hash brown potatoes I have ever tasted, fresh cantaloupe and cranberry muffins.

It hit me: My little girl, the baby of the family, is a 23-year-old honors graduate from East Carolina University making plans for graduate school. How in the world did that happen?

We had a lovely June breakfast, a morning filled with laughter and love. And then they left, back to their own worlds, back to worlds where they are strong, independent women and not some blubbering old Dad's little girls.

The gifts we dads got this year were nice, but the best gift of all was the sure knowledge that no matter what else we have failed to do in our lives, we did one thing very well: We helped give the world some terrific people. And there are never enough of them to go around.

But like a lot of dads whose children have grown up, I sort of missed the runny eggs.

Mr. Wonderful for Real

I have been at it for 23 years, and I still haven't decided if being the father of daughters is a blessing or a curse.

On one hand, we daddies get to be the dashing hero who can leap tall buildings in a single bound to at least one human being in the world. There is nothing Daddy cannot do. While we grumble that, hey, we're only human and go ask your mother, we really like being a brave, strong Daddy with all the answers. Our role is sort of like the cavalry of the parental team, riding to the rescue of our very own little damsels in pigtails when danger lurks. That is the blessing part.

But once you get past the skinned-knee stage, things can get difficult.

Now I've been hearing about this wedding business for several months now. Some guy really thinks he's good enough for my daughter? Surely you jest. I mean, he's merely flesh and blood. I expect much more from the man who takes my daughter's hand.

I've met the young man. He seems like a nice enough fellow, and I am fond of him. But, marry my daughter? Is he kidding?

I made the mistake — and I have paid for it — of thinking this would all somehow magically blow over and I did not have to concern myself with the gory details. Hey, she got over it when Donny Osmond got married, didn't she? Young Mr. Osmond once had been destined to father my grandchildren.

I figured the current Mr. Wonderful would one day become Mr. History. I listened with half an ear as she told me her wedding plans. I nodded and smiled a lot. How cute. I remembered Donny and David Cassidy, too. I didn't really believe it would ever come true.

The woman was not kidding. And this is the curse part.

Hey, Dad! Yeah, you, sitting there reading the paper. I hate to be the one to break it to you, but you've got one of the great shocks of your life coming. And there is no way to prepare for it. It is as sudden as a cinder block dropped on your head.

It is called Picking Out the Wedding Dress.

Her mother had been on a semi-crying jag for days. She had had the pleasure of escorting our eldest all over town, and her report to me was filled with lots of snorts and sniffles. They had visited numerous shops that sold wedding dresses, and what had begun as a simple shopping trip had turned into one of the emotional traumas of that mother-and-daughter relationship.

They had found the perfect wedding dress. And every time I heard about it, the report was increasingly tear-stained.

Silly women, I said, crying over a bunch of white material. Not me, boy, not Mr. Cool. Yeah, sure, she's getting married. Wedding dress, right. Sure, I'll go look at it. Big deal.

Then my little girl walked out of that dressing room in that one perfect wedding dress, and I died inside.

My little girl wasn't a little girl anymore.

I knew she was already grown. One look at the calendar proved she was 23 years old. I knew all that in my head — but not inside, not where it matters. In there, she is forever 13.

But one look at her in that wedding dress — a dress that costs more than twice what her mother and I paid for our first car — and I knew in my gut that it was all over. She really is going to get married.

I just sat there with a stupid grin on my face, wishing I could turn back the clock about 10 years.

And I'll have to go through it again, because I've got not one but two lovely daughters.

Lucky me.

The Pulse of Life

We do some dumb things when we're scared.

I was in a Raleigh department store trying to decide whether I wanted the black pajamas with the red piping or the gray pajamas with the maroon piping. The choice seemed both difficult and important.

It then occurred to me, as I stood there on the hot afternoon of

July 3, that I might die in these stupid pajamas and it didn't really matter what color they were. What mattered was that I hurry my ailing body to the hospital like the doctor said.

So I bought the gray ones (the black ones looked like they came from a brothel) and charged them. If I lived, I'd pay for them. If I didn't, well, the retail business is a daily gamble.

I lived, so now I guess I have to pay for the pj's.

"Dennis Rogers is ailing" is the way the paper put it. "Dennis Rogers is lying in a hospital bed paying real close attention to each and every eagerly anticipated heartbeat" would be more accurate, if a bit wordy.

The doctor called it "ventricular arrhythmia."

You know that feeling you get when you're lying on the beach and the most incredible body you've ever seen is slowly strutting past, and just as your fantasies reach the boiling point, and that little smile turns up the corner of your mouth, your spouse — who you thought had gone for a walk — snarls, "What are you looking at?"

You know how your heart seems to skip a beat?

That's what ventricular arrhythmia feels like. The difference was, I had been sitting at my desk on a Saturday afternoon writing a column about sailing with the Navy. The beach was 150 miles away, and the only thing strolling by was my boss. It seemed an uncalled-for reaction.

One skipped beat I thought I could overlook. We do tend to stick our heads in the sand sometimes, don't we? But after three days with the skips coming every minute or so, the doc decided I should check in before I checked out.

So there I lay, in the seriously sick department, wired to a machine just like on TV that went "beep, beep" and showed a green blip on a screen every time my heart decided to beat. We turned the sound down, and I tried not to look at the screen. If a fuse had blown in that machine, I would have died of fright.

My friends and family were real nice during my ailment.

My kids came to see me. Great, huh? The family pulling together and all that? It turns out they'd been over at my house making some preliminary decisions on the possible redistribution of my record collection. Two friends, who have started their own business, laid claims to my beloved T-bird as a company car. Another friend wanted to move into my house when I went to that big newsroom in the sky. Thanks, guys.

My hospital stay did have its moments. Our group has a tradition of getting together on the Fourth for an afternoon-long cookout, followed by watching fireworks from the Meredith College lawn.

Being wired for sound in the hospital, I was not able to join them. They all came by early in the day for a brief visit and then took off, with unseemly haste I thought, to go party on the deck. I was feeling lower than a snake's navel when, out the hospital window, I spied my friends staging the First Annual Rex Hospital Fourth of July Parade.

They arrived, appropriately, in the back of a pickup. They piled out, unrolled a banner that wished me a Happy Fourth of July, unfurled a large flag and marched around the parking lot. Then three of them sneaked into the hospital bearing two hamburgers and a cold bottle of ale.

It was the funniest thing I've ever seen. I laughed until I had tears in my eyes. At least, I'll always claim they came from laughing.

I am fine now, thank you. My erratic heartbeat is slowly getting back to a regular "thump-thump" from its recent "thump-thumpty-thump . . . thump," and in many ways I feel better than I have in years.

A friend asked me how I'd enjoyed my trip. What trip, I said. I've been in the hospital. Don't you read the paper? I've been ailing.

"Ailing?" he said. "I thought it said sailing."

Happy Madness of Theater

Sunday schoolers do it every Christmas in every church, and proud parents beam. Tough-as-nails combat veterans at Fort Bragg do it between missions to the world's trouble spots. More movies have been made about it than any subject except love and Westerns.

Some people have become rich and famous doing it. Others have lost their shirts.

It has broken up marriages and made people fall in love.

It is done in expensive silks and brocade and in the nude.

It can cost a million dollars or not a dime.

It is the most uplifting, depressing, relaxing, exhausting, thrilling and boring endeavor in which humans take part.

It is community theater.

No one knows when those fateful words were first spoken: "Hey, I've got an idea! Let's put on a play!" But as surely as there is a need for food, shelter and sex, there is an intense need in a lot of people to stand up in front of an audience and perform.

I am one of those people. This summer marks my 17th year as an actor in community theaters across the state. The last count shows that I am in my 31st production, and my interest is casual compared with that of thousands of folks across Eastern North Carolina.

For example, summer is a slow time in community theaters. People are on vacation and farming and doing all the things they do to have fun in the summer. Yet 14 plays were noted in the calendar listing of The News and Observer Sunday. They ranged from a play celebrating Sampson County's bicentennial to the show I'm in ("Finian's Rainbow" at the Raleigh Little Theater) to the nation's oldest outdoor drama, "The Lost Colony," in Manteo.

There is nothing quite like it.

I first walked into a theater at Fort Bragg during the summer of 1967. I saw a notice about auditions and went in out of curiosity and boredom on a slow Sunday afternoon. I sat on the back row and watched for a few minutes, and the feeling that has kept thousands at it for almost two decades hit. I watched the would-be actors on stage and thought: "I can do that."

I couldn't or at least not very well, but that didn't stop me. I borrowed a script and gave it a shot and won a part.

Community theater is the magic and flash and dazzle that can make a good community a great one. It takes thousands of hours of hard work interrupted by brief moments of sheer joy to put on a play.

It is all done by volunteers. Volunteers build the sets, they make phone calls by the hundreds to sell season tickets to pay the outrageous bills and they sew the hundred or so costumes that the average musical needs. They memorize long scripts, rehearse for long weeks and sweat bullets every night before they walk on stage in front of their neighbors. They give up their vacations to run spotlights and never share in the applause. They say they will be there, and they are, no matter what happens or how bad they feel or how tired they are.

Yes, it is true; the show must go on.

It rained on our outdoor preview performance last week, and we stayed out in the rain. We spoke our words and sang our songs, our costumes dripping wet, our spirits as low as the clouds. We started late because someone had stolen our lights, and by the time it was over, it was early Thursday morning.

But the magic was there because when we finished, an audience as wet and bedraggled and tired as we were sat under their umbrellas and applauded for us.

The magic is always there. You begin with a bare stage and a script that is nothing but typewritten words on paper.

It seems that it will never work. Lines are hard to learn, and the fear of standing out on a stage and forgetting those lines — that black terror that hits so hard you couldn't even remember your name if you had to — makes you shake and wipe your sweaty palms before every show.

We tried to work outside in one of the rainiest Julys in North Carolina's history. Rehearsal after rehearsal was rained out. We worked until midnight, night after night, and then got up the next morning and went to our jobs, only to do it again the next night.

We have taken no vacations, seen no movies, spent no weekends basking by the pool or playing at the beach. We have abandoned our families and our social lives. One of our cast members who runs a construction company took his crew of workers away from a paving job to the theater to help finish the set before opening night, and he paid them out of his pocket.

And it isn't just us; it happens across the state. Our experience is only typical.

Why do we do it? We do it for the friendship of fellow actors and technicians, a funnier and brighter-than-average group of people. We do it because it is fun to take a piece of wood and a can of paint and create a fairy land. We do it because it is fun to take a typewritten work and speak it so it makes people laugh or cry.

We do it because on opening night, after the weeks of drudgery, when the lights are shining and the music is swelling and the sets are glistening and the costumes are ready and the words are all learned, the curtain goes up and our friends and neighbors are entertained. They forget the real world for a couple of hours, and we take them to a world where the good guys win and the gal always gets her feller.

It is magic, and we do it.

When the lights come up full at the end and the applause builds and we stand there, smiling our silly grins, we are paid in full.

When the Bikers Meet

Wampee, S.C.

The groom was dressed in white, and the bride was dressed in morning gray — a reversal of the way most couples suit up for marriage.

But the "preacher" had shoulder-length hair, a chain wallet and a leather vest. The bridesmaid rode around the outdoor wedding site on the back of a thundering motorcycle, waving her bouquet while thousands of motorcycle riders cheered.

Welcome to the 47th annual Harley-Davidson Spring Rally, the all-out, good-times unofficial beginning of summer for Tar Heel bikers.

Staged each year by the N.C. Harley-Davidson Dealers Association, the gathering drew about 10,000 bikers to the Grand Strand of South Carolina for a weekend of parties, bike shows, games, drag races and a renewal of the brotherhood of bikers.

It was time to wipe off the winter kinks, polish the chrome, fire up the bikes and run to the sun.

As we pulled out into the morning traffic at 7:15, there was some doubt and a lot of wet drizzle on our goggles.

Thirty-four bikes rode together from Raleigh. That might not sound like many, but by the time we were spread out in a safe riding formation, the front of the pack was lost in the fog.

Our pit stop in Spivey's Corner is one I'll long remember, at least until the scab comes off and I can sit comfortably again.

We had just pulled away on the second leg of the trip when I felt the clutch cable give way with a solid snap. No problem, I'll pull over, we'll grab a new clutch cable from the box of spare parts that local dealer Ray Price always carries in the van that hauls luggage, and we'll be under way again. No big deal.

It is amazing how slick wet grass on the sloping shoulder of the road can be.

I got my Wide Glide almost stopped, but then physics took over. I hit the brakes lightly, but the rear tire slid on the grass and motorcycle and skinny biker went every which way.

I laid down the bike with no problem, but those riding behind me said it was the funniest thing they'd ever seen. Then I slipped on the grass and sat down on the hot exhaust pipes.

I came up real quickly. But not quickly enough. My riding buddy Danny Luder had the clutch cable fixed in no time, but when I sat back down on that seat, I knew Myrtle Beach was going to be a long, uncomfortable ride down the road. I was right. But the pain in my seat did distract me from the throbbing of my right knee, which had hit something hard in my crash ballet.

Even so, it was a delightful ride on a Carolina spring morning. The scent of honeysuckle was thick as we headed south. It blended with the morning sun that greeted us near Whiteville and flavored the smell of the new fields we were riding past.

I must admit that I spent most of Friday afternoon sitting gingerly by the pool while others cruised the streets of Myrtle Beach, checking out the bikinis and other bikes.

Saturday was the big day. The dealers had rented a drag strip near the small town of Wampee, and by noon 10,000 motorcycles were inside, while their riders and their ladies strolled around looking at expensive show bikes and watching and playing biker games.

It has been said that bikers have more fun than other people, and it might be true. The potato scramble is always a favorite. Bikers ride in a big circle. After a signal, they stop and their ladies jump off of the back and race to a big pile of hay in which potatoes are hidden. But there is one less potato than there are ladies, so one comes up empty each time. The struggle not to end up empty-handed is fun to watch.

It goes on until there is one potato and two ladies, and a cash prize awaits the winner.

There are slow races — try riding a big, heavy Harley across a grass field as slow as you can without putting your feet down and you'll separate the serious riders from the weekenders like me.

And there's the hilarious weenie bite.

A hot dog smeared with mustard is hung from a beam as bikers ride beneath it. The lady on the back has to reach up and take a bite from the weenie without using her hands. The losers drop out, and the weenie is raised each time. It can get messy.

Sunday was time to pack up and head home. We said goodbye to friends we hadn't seen in a year, mounted up and joined the flood of other bikers leaving town.

We left behind some good memories and about a million dollars in Myrtle Beach cash registers.

It is a good feeling to be riding with friends whom you know you can count on. I knew there was no way I'd be left by the side of the road to take care of my broken clutch cable alone. Thirty-three bikes would wait patiently for me, as they would again Sunday when my friend Bob McHose blew a tire near Tabor City.

It is that feeling of brotherhood, of being able to count on each other, that makes riding to the Spring Rally so much fun.

Road Brother Riding Free

Fayetteville

I remember the first time I ever saw Little John. He was a short, sort of grizzly, smiling one-eyed man on a mission of mercy in a white pickup truck.

It was a Sunday afternoon in Kinston. Several of us had taken a motorcycle trip to a biker party and were heading back when the battery on my then-new bike gave up and quit. Being a hundred miles from home with a dead motorcycle beside the road on Sunday afternoon is a nervous time, but the incident taught me something about biker brotherhood and Little John Newton.

Bob Ray from Wendell was along on the trip, my first as a member of the Concerned Bikers Association. We fiddled with the bike for several hours, trying to coax life into it with no success. Finally, as darkness began to fall beside the road, we called Little John for help.

Little John didn't know me. I was a brand new member of the group that he'd been a member of for years, and we'd never met. But that didn't matter. I was a brother in trouble, and he came to help.

He left a family backyard cookout that afternoon and drove two hours from his home in Clayton. We loaded the bike in the truck, and by the time we got to my house, got the bike unloaded and he got back home, it was midnight.

I tried to thank him, to pay him for his gas, to do something to let him know how much I appreciated what he'd done for a stranger. He wouldn't take a thing but a handshake.

We buried Little John last week.

We did it the way he would have wanted it. Five members of our group rode their motorcycles from the funeral home in Clayton to the graveside services in Fayetteville. We went to the funeral in our boots, jeans and leathers, the riding clothes we'd worn so often when we rode with Little John. And we carried him to his grave while the better-dressed friends in suits watched.

He died on his bike on a Saturday night less than a quarter of a mile from his home. Somehow he ran off the road and hit a ditch and a sign.

Little John was a good friend, a good biker and a good man. Over the years, we've raised a lot of money for charity, and John was always there to help, whether it was shoveling coal for Warmth for Wake or helping run the bicycle races at Lions Park or manning a stop at our frequent charity poker runs.

He worked for the forest service in North Carolina. Little John ran the nursery at the Moody Clemmons State Park near Clayton, where he once estimated that he'd raised more than 1 million pine trees to be planted across the state. The large wreath that lay on his coffin came from those pine trees, and it seemed fitting.

We mourned the loss of our brother, but in our fashion, we spent most of the time telling funny stories about Little John. The funeral was over, the final words had been said and everyone but our little band of bikers had left the grave site. Still we stood there, talking of Little John in the afternoon sun, a day that was just perfect for riding, the kind of day he would have loved.

Bruce Harris told about Little John's new boots. Bruce, his wife, Vickie, and Little John were hanging out at TC's Lounge one day when Vickie and John got to talking. One thing led to another, and before Bruce could warn Vickie that she was surely going to lose her money, she bet Little John $100 that he wouldn't drop his pants right there in the bar.

She should have known better. If she'd known Little John, she'd have never made the bet.

He stood up, loosened his belt and dropped his pants to his ankles and laughed. She paid up, and Little John used the money to buy a fine new pair of riding boots.

He was wearing those boots when he died, and his wife, Carol, intended for him to be wearing them when we laid him to rest.

But Little John had a daughter named Ada and a son all of us called Weezer, and Weezer wanted his daddy's boots. And he got them.

Those will be tough boots to fill, Weezer. Your daddy was a good man. His brothers stood there that afternoon thinking about John. There was Bill Becker, Charles Boone, Bruce Harris, David Gore, Tommy Hall and me.

Some of us had left private mementos to be buried with him. As we walked away, someone said, "It just won't seem right without Little John.''

He was right. All of us have lost a brother we knew we could count on.

Ride free, Little John, and thanks.

Still Another Biker Death

And now we've lost two.

There must be some reason for it, some great meaning that we can't see. But if it is there, we haven't found it yet.

I just told you about the good life and tragic death of my friend John Newton. On a Saturday night in October, less than a quarter of a mile from his home in Clayton, Little John somehow lost control of his motorcycle and died.

One of the pallbearers at Little John's funeral was a tall, easygoing, easy-smiling friend of all of us named Tommy Hall. He and Little John were close friends and riding buddies, and it was right that Tommy, a 39-year-old Raleigh brick mason, help take Little John to his grave.

But just 16 days later, it was Tommy who died on a motorcycle.

I guess we'll never know why Tommy died. For some reason, he got on his motorcycle on a beautiful Monday afternoon and minutes later, traveling at high speed, crashed and died on Atlantic Avenue.

We who ride motorcycles pay attention when one of our own dies. We know, I guess, that it could have been us. Many of us saw the evening television news reports or heard the radio reports that Monday afternoon and we wondered who it was who had died. I saw the wrecked motorcycle on television and it looked familiar, but still I wondered.

The early reports said the biker had been traveling between 80 and 100 miles per hour when he crashed and, frankly, I quit worrying. My friends don't ride like that, especially on a busy city street on Monday afternoon.

But even if I'd known it was a friend and I'd had to guess which one it was, Tommy Hall would have been the last name I would have guessed. We teased him often about being Tail End Tommy, always the last rider in the pack when we went somewhere.

But it was Tommy. Our phones rang all night as we spread the word through the network. Gentle Tommy, always around but always in the background, was dead, and we, our little band of brothers already shaken by the death of our own, had to gather again and bury another one of our friends.

Facing the death of friends does not get easier with practice. It only gets harder. Shock and grief, it seems, are cumulative.

We gathered as before, in our leathers and jeans, but something was different. We were shocked when Little John died but sudden accidents happen and we handled it well, I thought.

But Tommy's death was different. This time there was stunned confusion in our eyes as we gathered again. What was happening to us? Why were we dying?

We buried Tommy on a bitterly cold day when the wind blew and the snow came. As before, we left our private mementos to be buried with him. There was a bandanna, a pin, his club patches.

Later we drank a toast to Tommy and we looked at each other in a way we never really had before. We told each other that the dying must end and end now, that we can't do this again. We've buried two of our small group in just over two weeks, and none of us want to go through it again for a long, long time.

But there seemed to be an unspoken fear hovering over us. Will we lose someone else? It is a common parting to tell a brother to ride carefully when he gets on his bike to leave you. We say it and we mean it, but the words, until now, have come automatically.

But not anymore. The snow was cold and the wind was still slashing as we parted that sad day but there was an urgency, almost a plea, in our parting words. We meant them like we've never meant them before. Ride carefully, we said.

We lost Little John Newton and now we've lost Tommy Hall, and we who remain will mourn them. We'll miss them most, I suppose, when the warm sun shines and the chrome sparkles and the engines are running smoothly and the road calls us to take a ride.

Ride carefully, my brothers. Please.

Time to Save the Nauga

I love this story that John Eckels of New Bern set along: "This is one of those stories that involve an uncle or a cousin, but it is always sworn to be true just the same. It may strike you as funny, as it did me.

"Prohibition never really came to my hometown in Ohio — not, at least, for a dozen or so special patrons of Louie's place.

"Louie ran what would have been called a saloon, except that saloons were forbidden during Prohibition.

"Louie, however, had a private pipeline to Canada across the lake, where the distilling of fine Canadian whiskey went on without much regard for the laws of the United States. As for beer, Louie brewed his own, down in the cellar. And good beer it was.

"Since the clientele included a number of grateful community leaders, including a judge or two, no federal agents ever interrupted operations. It is true that there were one or two threats, but tip-offs from local police gave Louie time to haul his crocks and bottles out of the shed. And when the 'feds' arrived, all they could find on the bar were a few bottle of "Moxie," an obnoxious soft drink popular only among children.

"From time to time, when Louie came by a batch of prime steaks or a haunch of venison, he whipped up a special treat to which all the regulars were invited. On the occasion which is the subject of this account, Louie not only got hold of the steaks, but a well-wisher contributed a peck of wild mushrooms, all of them prize specimens with caps a full two inches across.

"The feast drew a capacity crowd. And when all but a few of the guests had departed, trailing compliments for the host, Louie made a confession to the few who lingered.

"He'd had some misgivings, he admitted, as to whether the mushrooms were edible or of some poisonous variety, but he had reassured himself by frying up a few and feeding them to his German shepherd.

" 'Oh, my God!' yelled a fellow who happened to glance out the back window. When the others looked, there on his back, feet straight up in the air and eyes glazed, was the unlucky dog.

"The remaining guests ran for their cars to head for the hospital and the stomach pump, while Louie began telephoning frantically to find those who had left earlier.

"The physician's wife reported that he was already at the hospital seeing a patient. Some others, fortunately, had gone directly home. One fellow was finally located at the apartment of his lady friend. It was well past midnight when Louie headed wearily back to clean up the place and found this note stuck in the door:

" 'Dear Louie, I'm sorry about your dog. He must have got hit by a car. You had a lot of people in your place, so I carried him out of the street and put him in the back yard because I knew you'd want to bury him. Charley.'

"Louie debated about telling his patrons, but only for a moment."

Socking It to the Major

Anyone who has ever had a boss they didn't like will sympathize with this story. And anyone who was ever in the military will instantly recognize themselves:

The story comes from Harry Severance of Wilson:

"I had been home from World War II for several years when I made a business trip to New York City. After completing my business, I returned to Pennsylvania Station to catch my train back to Wilson.

"While walking through the terminal, I suddenly remembered that my wife had told me to buy a certain brand of socks from a certain New York department store. I was angry at myself for having forgotten, and so I looked around the terminal to find a clothing store.

"I saw one, looked at my watch and hurried inside. A man was standing in the front door and when I asked him where the socks were he said, 'Go straight down this aisle and you will find them.'

"I walked hurriedly down the line of counters, and as I approached the end I noticed a clerk who was leaning against the counter looking at me. I stopped, looked down into the show case where the socks were and said, 'I'll take a pair of these and a pair of these' while pointing at the socks I wanted.

"The young man never responded, just kept looking at me. I really didn't think he heard me so I repeated my request in a much louder voice. He never moved and just continued to stare at me.

"I was hasty with him and said, 'Do you work here?' and he, continuing to look at me, nodded his head in the affirmative. I then looked at my watch to make a point with him and said, 'I must catch a train in a few minutes so please give me my socks.'

"With that statement, he said his first words to me: 'Is your name Severance?'

"As one can well imagine with a name like Severance it is very difficult for even friends to remember how to pronounce my name and here in a city of some 9 million people, a complete stranger asks me if my name is Severance.

"I turned my attention back to this young stranger and replied, 'Yes, my name is Severance.'

"He then began to question me.

" 'Were you the Severance in the 70th Infantry Division when we were fighting in Germany?'

"My answer was yes.

"He then said, 'Major, you don't remember me?' and I said no, I didn't.

"He then said, 'Major Severance, I was Corporal Brown in the

275th Infantry until you busted me to Private Brown. Now Major, I have been waiting 10 years for you to come to this store to tell you to buy your damn socks from somebody else.'

"I enjoyed this scene so much that I really didn't care whether I missed my train or not."

Death of a Bull

This item comes from J. Reginald Collier of Roanoke Rapids.

"Here is my true story swap for the kick that I got from your recent mule article. It brought back old memories, not altogether fond.

"I was raised on a farm and in the store my father owned. There was open range, and foraging animals and fowl were — like horse manure — everywhere. The farmers had to fence in their fields.

"The railroad fenced in their cuts and depended on their screaming steam whistles to clear animals from the tracks. Now and then an animal was killed, and they paid a modest sum.

"We had a bull yearling. He was beginning to feel his oats. He was mean. When we boys got near he would whirl around, curl his tail, paw the ground and hook his horns. He was the meanest bull I every saw. We gave him a wide berth.

"One day the section foreman for the railroad came in and told my father that the train had killed the bull. My father filed a claim.

"Came the reply: 'Dear Sir. We have investigated the death of your bull. Our crew says that your bull got in the middle of the track, curled his tail, pawed the ground and had a fight with our train. We won. We decline to pay.' "

Straddling the Fence

Joe Curry, who runs a bed-and-breakfast inn in Wilmington, sends this along:

Politicians have been known to straddle the fence when faced with a controversy that could cost them votes no matter which way they go. This letter is a humorous take-off on their double-talk:

"Dear Friend," it begins. "I had not intended to discuss this controversial subject at this particular time. However, I want you to know that I will not shun a controversy. On the contrary, I will take a stand on any subject at any time, regardless of how fraught with controversy it may be.

"You have asked how I feel about whiskey. Here is how I stand on the question.

"If, when you say whiskey, you mean the devil's brew, the poison scourge, the blood monster that defiles innocence, dethrones reason, destroys the home, creates misery and poverty, yes, literally takes the bread from the mouths of little children; if you mean the evil drink that topples the Christian man and woman from the pinnacles of righteous, gracious living into the bottomless pit of despair, shame, helplessness and hopelessness, then certainly I am against it with all my power.

"But if when you say whiskey, you mean the oil of conversation, the philosophic wine, the ale that is consumed when good fellows get together; the drink that puts a song in their hearts and laughter on their lips and the warm glow of contentment in their eyes; if you mean Christmas cheer; if you mean the stimulating drink that puts the spring in the old gentleman's step on a frosty morn; if you mean the drink that enables a man to magnify his joy and his happiness and to forget, if only for a little while, life's great tragedies, heartbreaks and sorrows; if you mean the drink, the sale of which pours into our treasury untold millions of dollars which are used to provide tender care for our little children, our blind, our deaf, our pitiful aged and infirm, to build highways, schools, hospitals and care centers, then certainly I am in favor of it.

"This is my stand and I will not compromise."

Back With Class of '36

While historians may mark the passage of time by calendars, catastrophes and conflicts, those of us who live ordinary lives remember more important things. The '50s, for instance, were not the years of the Red Scare, the Korean War and Eisenhower, but the time of rock 'n' roll, coonskin hats, "The $64,000

Question" and the first appearance of Hula Hoops.

George Seastrom of Cary, Class of 1936, just got back from his 50th high school class reunion and brought back these thoughts on growing up and growing old in America:

"High school reunions can be a competitive sport. At early reunions, classmates compete with each other about jobs and incomes; at the 25th, it's spouses and children. After that they brag about their grandchildren and vacation and retirement homes while regarding, with envy and glee, classmates' waistlines, hairlines and wrinkles.

"It is said there are Three Ages of Man: Youth, Middle Age and 'You Haven't Changed.' But change is the name of the game. Consider: Graduates of the Class of 1936 were before The Pill and the population explosion which, inexplicably, went hand in hand.

"We were before television. We were before penicillin, polio shots, antibiotics, Frisbees frozen food, nylon, Dacron, Xerox and Kinsey. We were before radar, fluorescent lights, credit cards and ballpoint pens. For us, time-sharing meant togetherness, not computers or condos; a chip meant a piece of wood; hardware meant hardware and software wasn't even a word.

"High school girls never wore jeans. We were before pantyhose, drip dry clothes, ice makers, dishwashers, clothes dryers, freezers and electric blankets. We were before Hawaii and Alaska became states and before men wore long hair and earrings and women wore tuxedos.

"We were before Leonard Bernstein, yogurt, Ann Landers, plastics, hair dryers, the 40-hour week and the minimum wage. We got married first and then lived together. How quaint can you be?

"In our time, closets were for clothes, not coming out of and a book about two young women living together in Europe could be called 'Our Hearts Were Young and Gay.' In those days, Playboy referred to J.M. Synge's hero of the western world, bunnies were small rabbits and rabbits were not Volkswagens. We were before Grandma Moses and Frank Sinatra and cup sizing for bras. Girls wore Peter Pan collars and thought a deep cleavage was something butchers did.

"We were before Batman, 'The Grapes of Wrath,' 'Rudolph the Red-Nosed Reindeer,' Snoopy, DDT, vitamin pills, vodka (in the USA), the white wine craze, disposable diapers, the QE I or II, Jeeps, the Jefferson Memorial and the Jefferson nickel.

"When we were in high school, pizzas, Cheerios, frozen orange juice, instant coffee and McDonald's were unheard of. We thought fast food was what you ate during Lent.

"We were before Boy George, 'Citizen Kane,' J.D. Salinger and Chiquita Banana. We were before FM radios, tape recorders, electric typewriters, word processors, electronic music, disco dancing, and that's not all bad.

"In our day, cigarette smoking was fashionable, grass was mowed, Coke was something you drank and pot was something you cooked in. We were before day-care centers, house-husbands, baby-sitters, computer dating and dual careers.

"In 1936, American schools were not desegregated, blacks were not allowed to play in the major leagues and the DAR would not allow Marian Anderson to sing in Constitution Hall. 'Made in Japan' meant junk and the term 'making out' referred to how you did on an exam.

"In our time, there were five and ten cent stores where you could buy things for five and ten cents. For just one nickel you could ride the streetcar or make a phone call or buy a Coke. You could buy a new Chevy coupe for $659 but who could afford that in 1936? Nobody. A pity, too, because gasoline was 11 cents a gallon.

"If anyone in those days had asked us to explain CIA, Ms., NATO, UFO, NFL, SATs, JFK, BMW, ERA or IUD, we would have said alphabet soup. We were not before the difference between the sexes was discovered, but we were before sex changes. And we were the last generation that was so dumb as to think you needed a husband to have a baby."

'No Excuse Sunday'

Getting up and going to church every Sunday morning is not that easy even for the truly devout, and it is pretty well impossible for the rest of us.

My friend Cleve Wilkie from Kinston, a popular guest preacher in churches all over the place, found the following notice in a Baptist church bulletin in Bailey:

"To make it possible for everyone to attend church, we will soon be having a 'No Excuse Sunday.'

"Cots will be placed in the foyer for those who say, 'Sunday is my only day to sleep late.'

"Murine will be available for those tired eyes from watching TV too late on Saturday night.

"We will have steel helmets for those who say, 'The roof would cave in if I ever went to church.'

"Blankets will be furnished for those who say the church is too cold and fans for those who say it is too hot.

"We will have hearing aids for those who say, 'The pastor speaks too softly,' and cotton for those who say he speaks too loudly.

"Scorecards will be available for those who wish to list all the hypocrites present.

"There will be 100 TV dinners for those who cannot go to church and cook dinner.

"One section will be devoted to trees and grass for those who like to seek God in nature.

"Finally, the church will be decorated with both poinsettias and Easter lilies for those who have never seen the church without them."

Valentine for a Father

I offer you this Valentine from Mrs. Charmaine Nation of Raleigh:

"My father was a quite simple man whose teaching was mostly done through example, not words.

"When my mother died he was left with eight children, one grown and seven ranging from high school to 4 years of age.

"His life was not without faults or shortcomings, but at the core of his being was love. His caring for others never stopped at only his family. It included everyone he met, from the waitresses at his favorite restaurant to the stranger in the line at the grocery store and certainly it included all children. His smile was quick and so was his willingness to help others.

"Throughout my life, friends often felt sorry for me because I grew up in a home without a mother, in a home without many niceties and less money.

"In my sophomore year, one of my friends came from a home with all of the advantages. I remember one day that she came home with me on my birthday, feeling sorry for me because there would be no decorated room full of friends, streamers and gifts.

"When we walked into my dining room, my father was waiting. He had set the table and cooked a less-than-perfect dinner for me. In the middle of the table sat a lopsided cake he had baked. My only gift was a beautiful card with a $10 bill inside and the words, 'Happy Birthday, Sweetheart, Love Dad' on the bottom. As my friend and I looked at each other through tear-filled eyes, she said, 'My father never does anything for me except sign a card my mother buys.'

"I knew which one of us was the luckiest that day.

"Two years ago my father died. As anyone who has ever lost a parent can tell you, it is difficult. Just as my father taught me through his life and through his actions, he also taught me through his dying.

"Although he was attached to what seemed like endless machines and was unable even to speak because of tubes, he would always manage a smile for those who needed it.

"My brother tells a story about how a young laboratory technician was feeling very bad after trying to find a vein in that poor, tired arm. Rather than becoming angry, my father reached over and patted her hand and smiled.

"I will always remember taking my three children in for what we all knew was a final goodbye. They were so tender as they gently held his hand and told tales of their everyday activities. Daddy would smile and squeeze their hands and show wide-eyed delight over new prospective boyfriends and home runs that had been hit. It was an effort on his part, I know, but I also know that he wanted to give them the chance to say goodbye. He left them with the memory of a gentle grandfather whose entire purpose in life was love.

"At 9 a.m. on February 14, 1985, on Valentine's Day, my father died with his hand in mine.

"On every Valentine's Day, when one of his eight children, 26 grandchildren or 12 great-grandchildren remember him, we remember not his death, but his love."

The Rules of the House

Everybody has them. Try as we might to be flexible and understanding, there are some things that just drive us all bonkers. Is there a woman in the world who does not get just a little crazy when her man leaves the toilet seat up and leaves beard clippings in the bathroom sink? And is there a man who does not quietly clinch his teeth every time his lady grumbles about it?

Rules that both sides can agree on can save a marriage. My wife and I were really getting on each other's nerves about our one-lane driveway. One of us was always blocking the other's car. The first in invariably seemed to be the first one to leave.

Early morning is a delicate time at best, and it was not made easier by an overly polite "Would you please move your car" while I was in my robe, deeply engrossed in my coffee cup and morning newspaper. It always seemed to be raining on those mornings, and she was not amused by having to come back in the house to get me to move my wheels. And driving your car in your robe is not all that much fun. Where would the neighbors think I'd been if they just saw me getting out of the car?

We came up with an unspoken rule to survive. I now park on the street, and she gets to park in the driveway. It is not fair, but it works. I do it, the same way I put the darned toilet seat down.

It is never too early to work out the rules we expect the other person in our lives to follow. Some fourth-graders at Aldert Root Elementary School here in Raleigh came up with some rules recently that they expect their future mates to follow. Some of these kids are on the right track. Others are heading for big, big trouble in the marriage game.

Sedeka Waters offered these rules for her marriage:

"Do not drink beer or wine in my face. Do not bring in more than three friends. Do not wear tight things. Do not kiss me in a public place. Watch the children when I'm not home."

I guess the guys won't be coming over to watch the game and down a few with Sedeka's husband, huh?

The fellow who ends up marrying Brandy Burnett had better not be a sports loving, sloppy couch potato who likes to sit in front of the tube and eat:

"Watch one football game a week. All meals are eaten in the dining room. No picking the cake until it's done. Don't leave the hair in the sink after shaving. Don't leave clothes on the floor. Don't kiss me in places like K-Mart. You should finish school. Don't lie to me. Always tell me the truth. Don't leave the TV on when you go to bed."

Brandy and Sedeka are clearly not going to put up with any mess from their men. I suggest that neither of them marry Noel Thompson. He's got some pretty strict rules for the woman he chooses to marry:

"Make my bed. Wash my clothes. Get a job. Watch the child. Do not be fat. Ask me before going anywhere. Get a car. Do not smoke. Always drive with seat belts. Sew my clothes. Clean the tub. Cook dinner. Be home before 9 p.m. Wash my feet everyday."

Noel, my man, you might look into the possibility of becoming a Marine Corps drill sergeant. You might some day find the lady of your dreams, but you'll have to look long and hard for her. I think the last woman who would be perfect for you died of overwork some time in the 1950s.

Craven Bridges has only a few simple rules, but they don't seem to be very negotiable:

"Serve steak once a week. Wash my clothes. Sleep on the left side of the bed. Iron my shirts. Go to hunting school. Do not smoke."

Craven, you'll do all right. Just get yourself an old-fashioned country girl, but you might want to hide the bullets to her gun.

Erin Allison is obviously looking for a well-groomed, well-behaved, house-broken, well-paid Yuppie. I would advise her to stay away from Craven. They wouldn't get along at all:

'No drinking. No smoking. No drugs. No killing animals unless they are poisonous. No earrings. Don't spend more than $100 a day. No long beard. No long hair. Make your own bed. Mow the grass. Hang up your own clothes. Sleep on the left side of the bed.

"Make a lot of money. Sweep the driveway. Help take care of the animals. Take care of the flag on the house. Clean out the boat. Clean out the cars. Help keep the pool clean. Never lie to me. Never go anywhere without telling me."

I wish Noel, Erin, Craven, Brandy and Sedeka a lot of luck in finding a mate who fits their demands. They are all going to need it.

One for the Tar Heels

This joke came from my buddy Jimmy Cole: It seems that a great ACC basketball fan had never had a chance to attend the ACC tournament. Finally, after saving and scrimping for years, he managed to come up with a ticket to all the games.

Unfortunately, he died on the Friday morning before the first game. He got to heaven and was met at the pearly gates by St. Peter.

"St. Peter, I've got tickets to the ACC tournament," he said. "Couldn't you let me go back for three days to see the games?"

"No," said St. Peter, "Once you're here, you're here for good, but we do have a lot of great basketball players up here.

"You see those guys over there with 'G' on their chest? They're All-American guards. And those guys with the 'C' on their chest are All-American centers. And the guys with 'F' on their chest are All-American forwards. We've got some great basketball up here."

"But who is that fellow with the big 'D' on his chest?" the fan asked St. Peter.

"Oh, him" said St. Peter. "That's God. He thinks he's Dean Smith."

Death on Christmas Eve

Some people have asked why I occasionally write stories about war and the people who fight in them. I have sometimes been accused of glorifying war by telling stories of these heroes from North Carolina.

The reasons are many. For one thing, North Carolina has a large number of active and retired military families, and they seem to enjoy them. And I enjoy talking to these ordinary men and women who have found themselves in extraordinary situations. I am repeatedly amazed and heartened that normal people can perform so bravely in wartime.

There is another reason best explained by a letter I received from Mrs. Earl Morris of Colerain. It is about the stories I wrote about Stanley Rehder and the men who went down on the troopship Leopoldville on the last Christmas Eve of World War II.

"After reading that article," she wrote, "I knew that my brother, Tech. Sgt. Luther McBee Laurence, who was in the 66th Infantry, died on that ship.

"My parents were notified in early January 1945 that he was killed on Dec. 24, 1944, when his ship was torpedoed in the

English Channel. Then as I read your column on Monday morning, my heart skipped a beat. After no word about what had happened on that tragic night almost 40 years ago, here was someone, Stanley Rehder, who had shared that terrible experience.

"I called Mr. Rehder in Wilmington. He told me a bit about what had happened on that fateful night.

"After all these years I shed a tear for my brother and all the others who were involved in that tragedy. Even though Mr. Rehder did not know my brother, I am grateful for having had the opportunity of talking with someone who was there."

That's one reason I write them. No one every took the time to tell Mrs. Morris what happened to her brother. Wartime restrictions prevented it. Now she know a little more, and she feels a little better.

Here is another reason I write them. This letter comes from Joseph Walker of Durham, who also survived the Leopoldville sinking:

"It is surprising to me how little we have ever read or heard about the whole thing. Naturally it was kept quiet until the war ended, but even after that I read only one short item and that's all.

"Lt. Rehder's account is amazingly accurate as I remember the facts. Like him I was also 22 years old at the time. Unlike him, I was an enlisted man and therefore one of the 2,200 he mentioned as being in the cargo holds.

"We were packed like sardines in the mess hall. Some of us were lying on the tables, some on the benches and some on the floor.

"We had been feeling the depth charges exploding off and on all day and had had some practice drills of going up and onto the deck just in case. So when the torpedo hit, we did not have to be told what it was nor what to do. After taking about three steps up the ladder, I looked back and saw one of my friends still asleep. I went back and woke him and we proceeded to the open deck as we had in our practice drills. We could see the lights of Cherbourgh some five miles away.

"The explosion was loud and vibrated the ship something awful. By the time we got on deck the ship had already begun to list to one side. We stood there awhile and just prayed.

"After awhile someone ordered us to go to a higher deck. Arriving there, we saw men swinging by ropes from the sinking ship to the destroyer Lt. Rehder spoke of.

"The water was really rough. Sometimes one ship would be two stories above the other and sometimes two stories below. Those of us who timed it right got over safely. Many were not so fortunate and ended up in the water or crushed between the ships.

"I was thinking it was 6 o'clock when the torpedo hit. I got off at 7, and it was 7:20 when the ship straightened up and one end went down. It hit bottom before all of it was out of sight, making it sink at a different angle. That makes it hard for me to understand why it was so long being found.

"The information as I remember it was that about one-third of those aboard were killed either by the explosion or by drowning, about one-third got onto the other ship and remained dry while about one-third were in the water and were rescued."

That's another reason why I write them. Here was a man who went through hell on Christmas Eve and no one knew about it but him. Now others can appreciate his sacrifice.

This final letter from John Lowry of Raleigh is yet another reason why I write them:

"I was an Army Cargo security officer aboard a ship unloading ammo in Cherbourg at the time. The Navy gunnery officer and I had just come out on deck from eating when the silent area was disturbed by whistles.

"It seemed within minutes that every vessel in the harbor was headed out toward the Channel. We learned later the next day that almost 1,000 men were lost when the overloaded troopship went down, a few because of the faulty use of life jackets, but most because of the frigid water.

"The next day the merchant marine galley crew came up with a tremendous turkey dinner, but few of us enjoyed it.

"I still think of Cherbourg every Christmas."

Glorify war? Never.

Glorify our warriors? Yes, for they are our friends and family, and they served us well.

Daddy's Little Girls

Becky Johnston of Raleigh is a good friend, and I usually don't run comments from my friends, but what she said about her father and my column on the sweet pain that comes when a father watches his little girls grow up and move out was perfect:

"I loved your column concerning Daddy's Little Girls growing up into women and the resulting adjustment fathers have to make. I thought you might be pleased and surprised to learn that daughters go through the same adjustment trauma.

"I think the trauma has become worse during the past decade or so as women have become more independent and assertive. We are not supposed to need the kind of help given to Daddy's Little Girls.

"You know me. Do you think of me as a reasonably mature woman? As an independent career woman with mature interests? Most people do and so do I — most of the time.

"However, the day the wasp the size of a hummingbird flew into my living room window, I immediately picked up the phone, called my dad and waited for him to come over and kill it. Now, one might say that I have an irrational fear of insects, but regardless of that fact, the Daddy's Little Girl reflex took over immediately upon seeing the wasp fly into the room, and I called without hesitation or thinking.

"When my car died in the Crabtree Valley parking lot on the opening night of 'South Pacific' (Becky is one of Raleigh's finest actors and played the lead in the Raleigh Little Theater production of the musical), did I call a service station? No, I called my dad.

"When I had an automobile accident in November, what were the first words out of my mouth? 'Call my daddy, please!'

"That's a small sample of the times this independent and assertive woman of the '80s turned unashamedly into Daddy's Little Girl. You see, we may grow up into women, but we still want to be Daddy's Little Girl. The broken chain on the bicycle turns into a dead battery. The skinned knee from riding your bike down that steep hill your father warned you not to ride down turns into a bumped head from a car accident. The homework in math that you could never do on your own turns into investment questions. The rose your dad sends you to soothe one badly bruised heart because 'He' asked 'Her' to the dance instead of you turns into the advice to stick it out a little longer because you both have to make adjustments even though your new husband does leave his socks all over the house and refuses to help with the groceries.

"Daddy's Little Girl hasn't grown up and disappeared; the problems and resulting needs have just changed.

"We would be fools to stop being Daddy's Little Girls. That is one of the most safe, secure, warming roles in life. Why should we want it to end?

"There is a very special bond between Daddy and his little girl, a bond that will always exist no matter how old that little girl is, no matter how independent. I can only say that there will always be a part of me, mostly in the heart and soul region, that hopes I will always be, to some degree, my Daddy's Little Girl."

Of Possums and Velours

Wortham Shifflet of Beaufort writes: "I read with great interest the article you wrote recently about the slaughter of the toads in England. My heart goes out to the wildlife whose well-being is of such vital importance to the English.

"My purpose in writing to you is the plight of the North Carolina possum, whose senseless slaughter should be of great concern to all Tar Heels who take pride in their wildlife.

"Scarcely a day goes by that, on any given 10-mile stretch, one doesn't see three or four or more dead bodies lying beside the road. Why continue this wholesale killing of an innocent creature who has never harmed man or the environment?

"If three carcasses for every 10 miles of road is the norm, then on the 58,784 miles of state-maintained road in North Carolina, there must be about 17,634 possums killed per day.

"Do we want them to go the way of the 'nauga' whose hides were used to upholster the fine furniture of the South until recently?

"How can this species survive this attack? Something has to be done now! All interested citizens should write the governor and their representatives in the legislature. I also suggest the formation of a committee to 'Save the Possum.' I suggest this committee lobby the Department of Transportation to set up a fund to continue the propagation of this noble creature before it is too late."

I have done a lot of research on this possum question and I have come to the unavoidable conclusion that the reason we see so many dead possums on the road is that the critters are actually very stupid.

You would think that after several million years of evolution, a possum could get the knack of crossing a road. But it is a little-known fact of science that on the very day that a prehistoric cave man invented the wheel (in a cave just outside the Beargrass town limits), the inventor ran over three possums while test-driving his invention. And the possums haven't learned a thing. They still go chugging across a big road and . . . Splat! Scratch another possum.

We should all be thankful that possums cannot fly or we'd find them dead on our roofs after they got hit by airplanes.

Now the "nauga" is another, sadder matter. This gentle, trusting creature has long been absent from our shores and it is tragic. It wasn't that long ago that the mark of a man with a fine set of wheels was a rolled and pleated Naugahyde interior.

A few years ago you could go into almost any of the fine mobile homes that grace our Eastern North Carolina landscape and be assured of seeing a black Naugahyde sofa with a matching chair, usually in a style referred to as "Mediterranean." It was fine stuff indeed and you could always tell the true Naugahyde from the imitation by the sound made when a sweaty fat person got up out of a chair or sofa covered with the stuff. I had both, and they lasted through two kids. It was a constant source of entertainment when portly friends visited on hot days.

But the brave "nauga" has disappeared, and I fear now for the velour. Velours are small, cuddly creatures with soft fur and they are being stripped naked in an effort to replace all the Naugahyde-covered sofas with velour.

The velour is the first cousin of the even-rarer creature called the Ultra, a being whose suede-like fur has become very popular for women's clothes.

Another of nature's wonders that has all but vanished from the landscape is the legendary Multicolored Double Knit, a marvelous creature that brightened up the drab forest with their none-too-subtle hues of You're Kidding Pink, Make Me Sick Chartreuse, Screaming Orange and the ever-popular Here Comes Another One Lime Green. There used to be lots of Double Knits around, but as the craze for leisure suits and stretch bell bottom pants reached epidemic proportions in America, these funny-looking creatures bit the dust. It can take a lot of Double Knit skins to make a pair of bell bottoms and a matching jacket for a size 48.

It is too early, scientists say, to judge the impact of the New Wave fashion on the still-plentiful herd of Spandexes roaming free in the New Jersey chemical wastelands, although dwindling supplies of Lycras do have some fashion hunters concerned. But they tend to be alarmists anyway.

Ship Fever Grows Acute

I'm beginning to get the feeling that sailors are like bikers. Most people think their choice of recreation is nuts, so they tell everyone who will listen (most often each other) how much fun they're having.

Witness this from Robert Macklen of Raleigh: "Here is a test to see if you will like sailing.

"Buy or borrow some cheap foul (or fool) weather gear. Get a roll of several fifty and hundred dollar bills. Put the bills in one pocket of the foul weather gear. Fix a peanut butter and jelly sandwich and put it in another pocket of the foul weather gear.

"Now take a cold shower with the foul weather gear on. When you can't stand the cold any longer, step out of the shower. The bills will be soaked and so will your sandwich.

"Flush the money down the toilet and eat the soggy sandwich.

"Now here is the test question: Did you enjoy what you just did?

"If you did enjoy it, you will love sailing!"

Small Towns and Big Towns

At first, I though Elmo Hassell of Columbia had a valid point about a column on my car breaking down in Edenton, especially my comment about being afraid it was "small-town rip-off time."

But when I think about it, I think he's wrong.

He writes: "I just read your article on lemons in Edenton. I must say I am glad things turned out OK for you.

"You react the same about small towns as do most people from large towns.

"I've always wondered why people react so. I'm from a small town about 30 miles from Edenton. I see people like you everyday.

"I've found small towns always willing to help people stranded with auto problems. I've made many trips to my auto parts store after hours or on Sunday to get a part for someone broke down from out of town.

"But I've also been in cities like Raleigh and Norfolk. Hey, break down in one of those places and see how much help you get. You'll be lucky to be back on the road again in a week. I don't think people in larger towns have the feelings for helping someone like they do in smaller areas.

"My advice to you is to visit more small towns and talk to their people, visit their businesses and get to know them. You'll find a whole new world most people never know exists.

"I could go on writing about this forever, although I know you don't have time to read a lot because you must have to beat the rush hour traffic home.

"Oh, I have to go home also. It will take me about five minutes to travel the four miles to my home where I know everyone within six miles each way. Can you say this about where you live?"

As a matter of fact, at the time Elmo wrote his letter, I lived 1½ miles from the newsroom in downtown Raleigh in a turn-of-the-century house seven blocks from the state Capitol.

My neighbors and I grow tomatoes and peppers in our backyards (I was lazy this summer and did not for the first time in three years), and you never know when you'll come home and find fresh vegetables somebody left on your front porch.

Oh yes, we have front porches, and we sit on them and speak to passers-by.

I keep an eye on my neighbors' houses when they go out of town, and they do the same for me.

I borrow my neighbor's tools without asking. He needed a tomato stake the other day and came and got it and told me a week later.

The point is that down-home hospitality and neighborliness have nothing to do with the size of the town. I've spent the past 10 years traveling to small towns, and I've found some wonderful folks in them. I also have found one or two jerks.

I've found in the big city of Raleigh some terrific people who'll do anything they can for you. I also have found one or two jerks.

We've got lots of neighborhoods where the grown-ups, the kids and the dogs all get together to have potluck picnics and parades on holidays. We take food to our neighbors who have had a death in the family just like you do.

The point is, we're all the same. There are city people who feel out of place when they get to a small town. They don't know anyone, and they've seen the unfair movies about small towns, and they react with suspicion.

Country folks sometimes do the same thing when they come to the city. They don't know their way around, and every face looks unfriendly to them.

We all feel comfortable and secure at home and a little cautious when we find ourselves in a strange setting, especially when we're in a mild crisis.

The small towns of North Carolina are pleasant places, but they are not Mayberry.

The big cities of North Carolina are pleasant places, but they're not New York.

You love Columbia, and I love Raleigh. Good for both of us.